CLARE NASH

Design your life

An architect's guide to achieving a **work/life balance**

RIBA Publishing

Published by RIBA Publishing, 66 Portland Place, London, W1B 1AD

ISBN 9781859469798

British Library Cataloguing-in-Publication Data
A catalogue record for this book is available from the British Library.

Commissioning Editor: Ginny Mills
Assistant Editors: Clare Holloway, Lizzie Silverton
Production: Jane Rogers
Designed and typeset by Sara Miranda Icaza
Printed and bound by Pureprint Group Ltd
Cover image: Clare Nash

www.ribapublishing.com

To all the wonderful people who have helped me along the way

ACKNOWLEDGEMENTS

CNA team members current and past: Lucy Holland, Julia Healey, Katie Reilly, Rebecca Sowler, Jaina Valji, Harry Cowley and James Nash, without you CNA wouldn't be what it is today.

Particular thanks to Jaina, Julia and Rebecca for their input on this book and ongoing business support.

Case studies: thank you to Office S&M, Harrison and Stringfellow, Invisible Studio, Transition by Design, Gbolade Studio, alma-nac, Pride Road Architects and POoR for agreeing to be case studies and for providing inspiration to others. Particular thanks to those who gave up their time to be interviewed – Hugh McEwen and Catrina Stewart, Su Stringfellow, Piers Taylor, Alex Towler, Tara Gbolade, Caspar Rodgers, Lisa Raynes, Shawn Adams, Larry Botchway and Ben Spry.

RIBA Publishing: Liz Webster, Clare Holloway, Lizzy Silverton and Ginny Mills, thank you for your honest feedback and support.

Birdies: thank you for your much needed wisdom, support and laughter over the years.

Chris Gardener: thank you for helping me climb out of tough times and for endless creative input.

Maggie Newton: thank you for your cheerful yet direct approach that always sets me right.

Liz, Lorna and Becky: thank you for always being there, your cheerful encouragement, tears and laughs.

James: thank you for all your support, love and useful thinking; without you I wouldn't be able to do any of this.

Felix: thank you for giving me so much joy and inspiration.

Mum and Dad: thank you for your support, listening ears and good advice.

CONTENTS

ABOUT THE AUTHOR

Clare Nash is an architect and founding director of Clare Nash Architecture, a radical, majority-female practice specialising in rural energy-efficient design. She is an RIBA Role Model, an architectural business lecturer at Oxford Brookes University and author of Contemporary Vernacular Design: How British housing can rediscover its soul (RIBA Publishing, 2016).

INTRODUCTION

This book is aimed at the person I was 10 years ago, newly starting up a practice. I had no clients and no savings. I had very little experience of domestic projects, having spent the previous six years working on public buildings. Recently completing Part 3 had put huge fears into my mind. I wondered, why would anyone willingly go it alone in this litigious and highly stressful industry with seemingly low financial reward and long hours in an office? And, yet, I did!

I set up my practice in the midst of the recession in 2011. I had recently been made redundant following a six-month research trip abroad for my master's dissertation. I was in a small amount of debt. However, I managed to find some freelance work, could then afford the insurance and while working as a dinner lady part-time I set up Clare Nash Architecture with some postcards in shops in the local area and a basic website. For a while I took anything and everything; none of it paid that well and I seriously undercharged for my services. Finally, I read stacks of business books, got myself a marketing strategy and started blogging – talking to my ideal client. Consequently, by September 2014 I had become an expert in the client's mind in my area of specialism. Three months after blogging seriously, I had a business boom. Then came employees and a doubling of my fees. Still more work came pouring in. The business went mad for a bit, I worked much too hard, made myself ill and thought: 'I need to do something to get my life back again, I didn't set up in practice to run myself ragged. Seriously, what is the point?'

This book contains all my knowledge of how to set up and run a successful, life-giving business, but it also explores reasoning behind the long hours' culture and how to challenge it if you are an employee. It contains a bonus chapter for students struggling with the time pressures of university and not looking forward to entering an industry that does not currently value itself well enough. It covers money mindset issues, finding your strengths and outsourcing your weaknesses, how to build a happy, productive, remote-working team, presenteeism and more. I have made many mistakes along the way and these are described in detail. I share lots of learning around fees, particularly. Hopefully you will not need to make the same mistakes I did.

It felt very lonely when I set up. I hope it helps to know that there is someone else out there with the same fears, making the same mistakes and still muddling through in a fulfilling way. There is much to gain in running your own practice – freedom and autonomy, working on projects you love with people you admire, being able to see more of your family and friends. For me, it is worth the hard bits and I describe my coping strategies throughout.

My extensive reading of business books is distilled through personal implementation and practise, helping you to apply it to your own experience in the architectural world. Few books cover the emotional side of running a business. It's like having a baby – there are huge highs and lows and I want to be honest about these. Besides this, I did have an actual baby, and this is the first book I'm aware of that includes a chapter on keeping a professional business going when you have a newborn to look after.

Throughout this book I refer to various authors, speakers and blogs. I have compiled them all into references at the end of the book for ease.

CHAPTER 1

How to be a business owner architect

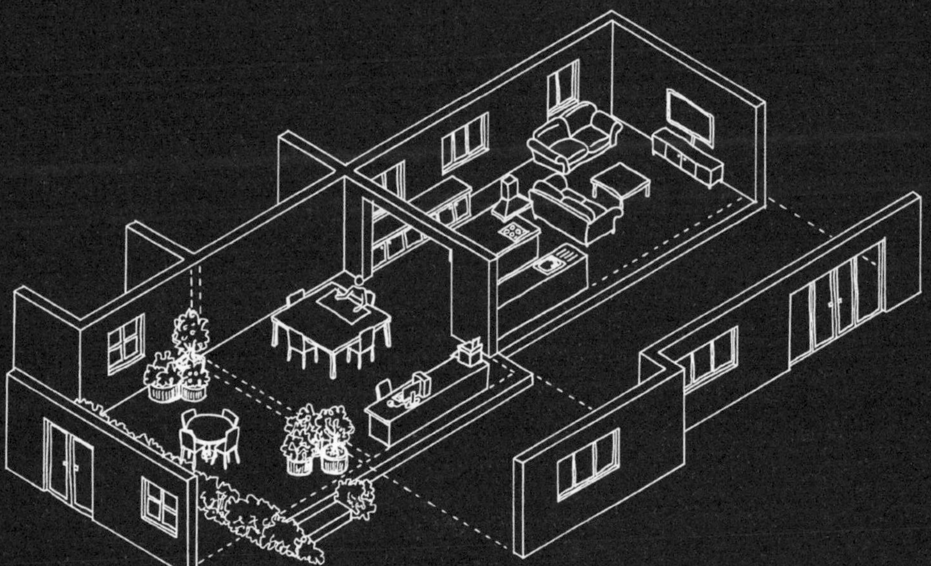

BENEFITS OF YOUR OWN BUSINESS

I won't pretend otherwise – running a business is hard. However, if you are entrepreneurial in spirit and prepared to think yourself out of problems creatively, it is very rewarding. I don't know of a single business owner in any field who hasn't had setbacks – sometimes enormous ones. The important thing is that they picked themselves back up again and made their business better. It's easy to believe when looking at Instagram or reading business leader profiles that they've had an easy road to success, but the stories that lie behind those pictures are quite different. I have personally found it very challenging in a good way, as well as a lot of fun overall, despite my own setbacks.

Below, is a list of benefits of running your own business in a way that suits you. As an architect, when earning low fees and without a separate source of income, these benefits are only short-term. It's possible to live for some time on low fees, just about paying your bills and enjoying your freedom, but sooner or later you will resent how hard you have to work and how much responsibility you take on behalf of clients.

- **Family:** this is a big one. It applies to anyone with caring commitments. Having my own business has enabled me to work around a tiny baby, not have to commute and pay enormous amounts on childcare, not have to put up with less exciting work just due to working 'part-time' in an office. Mainly, it has allowed me to feel a big part of my son's life without having to give up my identity to do so.
- **Set your own path:** I explain in Chapter 3 how I have always been very interested in eco-design. It felt extremely frustrating not to be able to push sustainable practice as much as I would have liked in practice. As a business owner, I can prioritise research and development in this specialist area, which is very fulfilling.
- **Other interests and business ventures:** at start-up stage, I had a sideline in German translating for a local clothing company. It helped to pay my bills and gave me the advantage of doing something I enjoyed without the pressure of making it into a full-time job.

FIGURE 1.1 Drawing of a working/pleasure trip I took to Brandenburg, Germany

FIGURE 1.2 Benefits of flexible working means still being able to work on projects such as this stables and barn conversion, even with a family

- **Working holidays:** when I am writing, I regularly escape for a few days to the sea to write. I also visit gardens, sit alone in a beautiful space and write or sketch out business vision ideas. I have previously worked from the Eurostar, an Austrian brewery, a Parisian café and even a boat!
- **Better use of time:** the Covid-19 pandemic has made the benefits of working from home familiar to many more people, but I have always enjoyed the benefits of using natural breaks to make bread, chop vegetables for dinner or go for a walk. Without any guilt. In winter, I appreciate the opportunity to enjoy bike rides or running in daylight. I was fortunate while working in Oxford that my office had a shower and was on the doorstep of great outdoor space, so I enjoyed regular daylight runs in winter, but not all offices have this. Since my husband joined the firm, we enjoy lake swimming together in the middle of the day (while our son is at nursery).
- **Other projects:** like 'other business ventures', above, one of the best things about flexible working is being able to fit in other projects around being an architect. After receiving the commission from RIBA Publishing to write my book, *Contemporary Vernacular Design: How British Housing Can Rediscover its Soul*, I set about organising case study visits, complete with designer, developer and resident interviews. Keeping my business going would have been impossible if I had needed to be in an office every day, as would holding down a job in a traditional architect's practice. My employers would have needed to be very enlightened and tolerant of me disappearing around the UK and Europe for up to 10 days at a time, multiple times, over a two-year period.
- **Legacy:** though possibly depressing for some, I find it uplifting to think about what my business may become without me, whether due to retirement, other interests or death. I want to create a truly sustainable business (in all senses) that lasts beyond my time on this earth.

DRAWBACKS OF YOUR OWN BUSINESS

Personally, there has only really been one drawback and that is the mental pressure on me as the sole director. I imagine it must feel easier as a partnership or a collective. Despite it taking me too long to realise this (see Chapter 7), I now draw on lots of help from my team, coaches, as well as my network of architects and consultants.

I do struggle sometimes to shut off easily in the evening/at weekends and focus on my life outside architecture. However, I don't think this is exclusively about being a business owner; it also applies to people with a job, so I talk about this more in the work/life balance section (see p. 102).

Pressure and Responsibility: staying sane and good mindset practice

The separation of my personal self from my work self has been a long process. When your business is essentially your baby and you have put everything into it, it is hard not to take it personally when something goes wrong. However, I am not my business. I created it, but I am not it. Over the years I have learnt to separate myself more and more. If things go wrong, I try to remember it is a small failure in the vast sea of enjoyable projects and personal and business growth that I have enjoyed. As humans we focus on failure rather than achievements. It takes practise to reframe and rebalance. There are lots of mental techniques to deal with this. Here are some that I use:

- I look at my 'vision or dream board', which is a collage of pictures of things I want in my life and inspiring quotes. It shows me where I am going and what it is all for. One step backwards is only a small hindrance in getting there. It is all worth the effort.
- The stars or the sea never fail to make me feel small and insignificant (in a good way). If you are small, it means your problems must be too. They will pass. It also often brings to mind the time I visited San Pedro de Atacama in Chile. Looking at the millions of stars in the Milky Way was awe-inspiring. I have always remembered the astronomer saying (in reference to astrology/horoscopes) 'the stars don't give a s**t about you'. And why would they? I remember this when I am anxious about a project. It is very liberating.
- I have a notebook in which I write all the good things that happen to me, be that a wonderful client testimonial or a lovely family day out or just a compliment. It really helps to flick back through that when times are tough.
- One of my business coaches, Chris Gardener, helped me to understand that my thoughts are just thoughts, they don't need to mean anything.
- He also taught me this: Think about the fact that you can have two people living in the same house with the same problems. One is more optimistic

and believes things will improve with a bit of time and energy; the other is very pessimistic and decides that they might as well give up because it's all going to fail anyway. Both people will be 'correct', because how you imagine your future is how it will become.

- I have had hypnotherapy. It has been really helpful to understand how certain beliefs could hold me back. I now have a few separate 'places' I can go to in my mind that help me to deal with problems. One particularly helpful vision is of me being very large, healthy and happy in the foreground. Far away is a tiny client. This helps me to understand that client or project problems don't need to take up so much space. My health is more important than any client.
- I garden. Gardening makes me feel closer to nature; I notice the seasons changing despite my troubles. Life carries on with or without you. That is very healing. Gardening is a form of creative activity; I get lost in it and again I am reminded of who I am, my overall reasons for being and that, no matter how big this problem feels right now, it will pass and I will carry on gardening.

The techniques that help you may be completely different. However, it is important to have those there as an arsenal to protect you when your times in business become rough – as they almost certainly will at some point.

THINGS YOU CAN DO TO IMPROVE YOUR LIFE AS AN ARCHITECT WITH A JOB

I think there are a number of factors that contribute to enjoying being an architect as well as having a life around it:

1. Autonomy over your life and work choices.
2. An interesting project work.
3. Feeling appropriately rewarded and appreciated.
4. Working at a practice that has morals and values that match your own.
5. Being effective.
6. Having time to enjoy family or friends outside work.
7. Having time for hobbies and other interests.
8. An ability to switch off after work or at weekends.
9. Feeling well.

You might already have some of these, or you might have none of these. The more you have, the happier you will feel at work. As a business owner I have all of these, most of the time, and I know my employees feel the same way. At times I don't feel rewarded enough for the stress involved or I fall back into bad habits of working too long or too late on projects without proper breaks. However, keeping tabs on these criteria helps to keep myself in check. So how can you get more of these things from your

FIGURE 1.3 Time for my allotment and for growing is part of the ethics of my business model

own place of work? First, I want to explain why architects particularly have a tendency to work too long and neglect many of the above in preference for 'great work' or career progression.

LONG HOURS CULTURE AND PEER PRESSURE

If you are the type of architect who just cannot get enough, who loves working every hour of every day on architectural projects, then that is fine. However, if you are not the incredible Zaha Hadid by nature, then read on.

The long hours culture tends to start at architecture school. Until recently, when mental health issues became more understood, universities embraced a culture of coffee and all-nighters. Just like fine art, there is a sense of never finishing a project. This can lead to never feeling good enough and to over-perfectionism, neither of which are healthy traits. I heard about one overseas boss (from a student intern) who made employees wait for his latest creative idea, whether that happened at 1am or 10am, because he couldn't possibly fit his 'creativity' into normal working hours. What is going on here? Yes, creativity can happen at any time at all, but others do not need to hang on to your every word. It can certainly wait until 9am the next morning. I mean, what an ego!

Presenting your work in crits in front of the people you most care about (your peers) is super-high pressure. You never forget that enormous fear of failure, of not being good enough, of always having more to work on.

The global pandemic has enforced a fundamental shift on how architectural practices work. I hope this leads to lasting change; particularly, that employers feel able to trust their team to work more flexibly. However, it is also up to the employee to take action. I regularly struggled with guilt, leaving the office at 5pm when others were still working but, overall, structuring my work like this had huge benefits on my efficiency, so no one complained. It is important to take action, not just expect an employer to provide this for you. Employers are busy people too; we need people to tell us when things need to change.

The long hours culture creates a vicious circle. You become less and less efficient because you are tired, and therefore need to work later and later to compensate. Not only this, but also your brain gets used to this schedule, so there is also no urgency around 4pm to complete whatever it is before you go home.

In this sluggish state, you are less likely to challenge poor business practice, even if you have an inkling that there is a better way. It is also a neurological fact that because we are pack animals, we do not like to stand apart from the group (we need to be accepted as part of the group because if we get booted out, we are far more likely to get eaten than if we remain part of the pack). You even have to override your prehistoric brain tendencies in order to make changes! All this is quite a tall order for any human, especially an overworked one keen to show commitment to their firm.

If you have children or other caring responsibilities, you may want to work part-time. I have done just that. However, it is notoriously difficult to find part-time work in architecture. I only hope that post-pandemic, finally we might understand that always being available is not essential. Collaboration does not need to be a constant background interruption; it can be more focused and useful.

Wanting to work part-time is not some kind of cop-out. It's also not just women who want this. In the 1950s there wasn't such a requirement for part-time working in architectural practice, as generally women stayed at home to look after children and, just as generally, the men did the architectural work. It is now 70 years later. Most households need two salaries to pay the bills and we all have to share caring responsibilities. Architecture can become an obsession at university, but as our commitments change in later life, we don't have to remain slaves to it. With a life outside an architecture bubble, we have an opportunity to understand the world around us and therefore our clients better. We make better decisions with more time to think away from the screen. There is no doubt in my mind that I am able to be a better architect because I also have a life outside practice.

In many ways, the computer has strangled creation. Of course, it allows more possibilities, but I can bet that your last great idea did not come about while staring at the screen. It was while walking, while sketching, while staring out of the window. How efficient do those long hours look now?

Ideas bring improvements in efficiency, happier clients (which means more repeat work), better design work and better buildings. However, I still have to remind myself of this and drag myself away frequently – even though it is a no-brainer from a business and health perspective.

In Germany, workers work hard between 9am and 5pm or 6pm (without social media distraction, which is generally frowned upon). They leave work feeling no pressure to stay behind 'because it looks anti-commitment if I leave on time', unlike in the UK. German school children first start school aged seven. In addition, there are more bank holidays and annual leave entitlement is higher than in the UK. Yet Germany is not producing sub-standard architecture. There is a greater celebration of life outside work; whole cities shut down to celebrate *Fastnacht* and various other events. People are not defined by their jobs in the same way as in the UK. I'm not suggesting the working world is perfect in Germany, but we could learn a lot from it in terms of our overall health and wellbeing.

Actions

None of these are easy; some actions will require bravery on your part. Some people find they are naturally able to ask for more, but for others it will require a lot of 'Wonder Woman' poses in the toilets first (see Amy Cuddy's TED talk[1]) or some support from colleagues. However, if you don't try, you will never know. It's highly unlikely you would lose your job just from asking for more. If you don't ask for more, you may find yourself leaving the job anyway. It's easy to focus on the negative consequences of standing up for ourselves (as per our pack mentality), but be clear on the negative consequences of not asking for more – e.g. poor health, needing to make a choice between architecture and family, not being able to afford a home of your own, or it could just be boredom. At the very least it will open up an honest conversation. Keep these in mind and it will help you to be braver.

AUTONOMY: FLEXIBLE WORKING

How many people at your firm would like to work flexibly or part-time? It is likely to be more than just you. Team up with them and prepare to call a meeting as a group and show your boss how this could work. There is power in numbers, and this will help to override the fear of standing out. Prepare a list of how flexible or part-time working will benefit the firm rather than be detrimental. Write a list of all the worst-case scenarios (e.g. builder needs a drawing today) and how you would deal with that. Then approach your boss armed with all the information.

INTERESTING PROJECTS

This comes from two things:

1. Moving practice if your employer doesn't engage in the kind of architecture that interests you.
2. If you have a particular interest in certain projects, say so. It benefits an employer to put people with enthusiasm on projects, because they will be highly motivated and solve problems faster.

REWARD: ASK FOR A PAY RISE

This takes preparation and you need a good reason why your company should give you a pay rise. Work out what is important to your boss and the firm, and how you would offer solutions or extra benefits in these areas. It can be hard to list your own strengths and skills, so ask a colleague to help (you could return the favour, which will give you both a morale boost). Everyone sweats prior to asking for a pay rise, so don't think it is only you who finds this hard.

PRACTICE MORALS AND VALUES

Do your research and wisely apply to a practice. If it's too late for that, look elsewhere with a clear understanding of your own interests and values. There are books to help on this (such as those listed on 'the School of Life' website: theschooloflife.com) or find a business coach or mentor. It is helpful to look back on past experiences. When were you most happy? What do others praise you for? In an ideal world, without money worries and commitments, what would you be doing? These are big questions and can feel uncomfortable. It is beneficial if you can work through them with a trusted person or a coach.

BEING EFFECTIVE

It's important to feel like we are good at something. Getting to know yourself better will help you to understand your strengths and weaknesses. Studies have shown that people are happiest when using their strengths. I still remember a story about tennis ace Boris Becker's coach. When asked if he would focus more on Boris's weak backhand, the coach said, 'No, I will make his brilliant serve even better.' Just as in sport, in business it is better to improve strengths further rather than focus on weaknesses.

Spending more time on the things you do well will also save you time. If possible, delegate your weaknesses to those who find it a strength. If you know what you are naturally good at, you can ask for more work in those areas. It can help to ask good friends and colleagues what they consider your areas of genius. Or you may find personality tests a good place to start. It is easier to see strengths in others than yourself.

TAKING TIME OFF

As a business owner, especially a sole trader, this can be very hard. If you work in the residential market, it is helpful to go on holiday when your clients do so. I always find it easy to take time off over Christmas and in August, because no one expects you to be working. Even builders stop. There's no pressure. You are not disappointing anyone (notice my trigger word there!). I still remember my first holiday without worrying about work. We went to Berlin and I felt that I could truly relax. Once you've had a taste of that, you want more!

If you are a sole trader, one thing you might worry about is missing enquiries and work. Engaging a virtual assistant (VA, a personal assistant/administrator working remotely) or an answer service to handle calls while you are away, send out questionnaires and set up meetings for when you are back, might help you to relax a bit more and not answer the phone on holiday.

As an architect in an office, it's important to make clear that you will not be answering emails or queries while you are away. People have their own different variations of what taking a holiday means to them. Some people seem to enjoy being 'always on' despite the health consequences. Don't expect others to read your mind. Make it clear and let them know where they can find everything in your absence. Write down potential dilemmas or queries that may come up while you are away and how to deal with them. Set up a project management board on Trello, as we do at Clare Nash Architecture (CNA), so it's not all stuck in your head. You really don't want to be taking work calls or queries about file locations from the beach. It's not a holiday then.

TIME FOR FAMILY, FRIENDS, HOBBIES AND INTERESTS: FILLING UP YOUR POT AND UNDERSTANDING YOURSELF

This is so important. If you are finding that these things are being pushed back in favour of long working hours, sooner or later you will feel like you don't know who you are anymore. We live in such a busy society, our commitments outside work can be many and varied, and fitting these in around work is challenge enough. However, spending some time doing a hobby that you love will make you feel like it's all worth it. A leadership coach friend of mine,

FIGURE 1.4 Taking time off is so important for creativity (holiday let conversion by CNA)

Aly King-Smith, often refers to this as 'filling up your pot'. Some work and commitments drain your pot, so it's important to keep topping it up with things that inspire you and make you happy. Otherwise, it's a quick route to rock bottom. Shorter hours and/or flexible working will help you to fit in more time for the things you love. Saying no to things you feel you 'should' do rather than things you love doing will give you more time as well.

SWITCHING OFF: SETTING BOUNDARIES

It's also worth reading the 'Separating work and home life' section in Chapter 9.

My father was a farmer and work was around him at all times. We didn't have many holidays and it was a big effort for him to leave the farm. However, we lived in a wonderful place, with lots of freedom and lots of space. I learnt that if you enjoy your work, it doesn't have to be clear-cut between home and work. Growing up like this meant that I always felt that I didn't need to earn a lot if I live in a wonderful place, because that is my reward. I also learnt that if you don't have good support, you can't go on holiday! I don't think always being available for work is a modern life thing, but it's harder for the average employee/person to escape, today. I think business owners of any kind and in any lifetime have always struggled with it.

In the past, there were physical boundaries between home and work. We could leave the office and forget about it until tomorrow. Nowadays you can easily bring work home via your phone. It is therefore important to set up virtual boundaries to achieve the same effect.

Setting up Virtual Boundaries

Here are some tips to help with this:

- This came from my structural engineer colleague: if you don't ask people questions on a Friday, they won't answer you at the weekend! This is quite a big breakthrough for me. I often try and clear my to-do list on a Friday afternoon, often in the form of emails. It is probably different with commercial clients, but domestic ones usually have more time at the weekend to email you. You don't want to encourage this. However hard I try, I often find that I 'accidentally' check email at the weekend. If it's a client answering your queries, it's very hard not to get sucked back into work mode. It easily nags you all weekend, sapping your energy and leaving you exhausted prior to the week starting again. 99% of the time you can't do anything about solving their problem until Monday anyway.
- You can have a work laptop and a personal one. Make sure your work email is only on the work laptop and nowhere else. It's much easier to glance at your phone than opening up a laptop and logging in, so this helps to create a barrier.
- Keeping your email online only (e.g. use Gmail interface instead of Apple Mail or Outlook). Again, the simple act of having to log in to check something means you are less likely to do it unless really necessary.
- It's so important to switch off regularly. If you are always 'on' not only are you always a little bit stressed but also you are missing out on fun-brain time: the part that has energy left over to think of fun things to do with your children/spouse/partner/friends/yourself. The part that has energy left over to have a life. Over time, ignoring this can lead to serious health issues.
- Turn off all your email notifications: all the noises and banners. Then you can choose to read them, you are in charge of it, rather than the other way around. As Chris Gardener (my mentor) says, email is all about other people's agendas, don't let them derail your own. It's good practice to do this with other work-related notifications too. On Slack (a messaging app for teams) you can set your working hours, which is very helpful.
- Train your clients to communicate with you, how you want them to. For me, client communication is always phone or email. I don't respond to WhatsApp/text/Facebook from clients. They soon get the message. LinkedIn is fine for contacts with whom I don't need to communicate that often. WhatsApp is a fun-space for me and my friends. I don't want to go in there at the weekend and see a client query at the top of the list. Ditto for text messages, although these are quite rare these days.
- I never answer the phone to anything work related after 6pm (mostly after 5pm). Some architects work later than usual hours to fit in around

childcare, so it might not be 5pm or 6pm for you, but you can educate clients to your own boundaries.

- I don't respond to email after 6pm (I might write a response if I will feel better afterwards or if I am in the mood, but I won't send it until the next day, otherwise you risk starting a conversation and/or they think this is a good time to catch you).
- I have worked for many years on developing a mindset that doesn't put me automatically at the bottom of the list. When a client says 'jump', I no longer say 'how high?' because, ultimately, this doesn't do me or my client any favours. If you are always firefighting, over-delivering, responding very quickly, you haven't got time for developing good health for your business or your body.
- Getting perspective on things can be difficult. Our human minds are trained to obsess over worst-case scenarios because this would have saved us from being eaten in our long distant past. This is not useful today. In fact, it can be quite damaging long-term. See the 'mindset practice' section of this chapter (p. 4) for coping strategies.
- See my weekly scheduling methods in Chapter 8 'Time-management systems'.
- Most of this requires setting boundaries with yourself first and sorting out your mindset. If you are in scarcity mindset (when you think there isn't enough work out there for you), then you will act desperate and respond out of hours to potential enquiries, existing clients and almost anything really. A scarcity/desperation mindset just repels clients. Who did you want to be more friends with at school? The cool, easy-going, fun kid or the desperate-to-be-your-friend kid?
- I have come to accept that the lines between home and work do blur sometimes. I am the same person doing both after all. I enjoy my work and sometimes I am very happy to work on parts of it that I most enjoy at the weekend. However, doing this too often means you are missing out on something else, so be careful what you prioritise. Moreover, make sure it is a choice rather than a necessity.
- During times of peak stress, I find myself anxiously checking email and social media after working hours. When I am calm, I switch off, knowing I have done my best for the day. Over time, I have started to understand how I need to feel in order to switch off. Cal Newport describes a great system in his book *Deep Work: Rules for Focused Success in a Distracted World*. He goes through all his checklists at the end of each day. For anything left unfinished, he makes a plan for when it can be done. This way the brain can more easily shut off; it's not trying to remember something you have forgotten. By making a plan for when you will get something done, your brain can relax, knowing that task is accounted for.

I won't pretend to have achieved some kind of holy grail of work/life balance. It is always improving, but the above items really do help.

STAYING WELL

Working fewer hours, prioritising things that make me happy, coaching/therapy, as well as the obvious things like good diet and exercise have kept me consistently well ever since I made myself ill through overwork in 2013/14. I have discovered that the simpler my life is, the happier I am. It took me a long time to understand that my wellness has to be a priority. My business would not succeed without it.

Long hours = something wrong with the business model

If you are working overtime (for free!) consistently, there has to be something wrong with the business model of the firm you work for. There could be many reasons for this, with some examples below:

- The practice is in a race to the bottom, competing with others just on price rather than value.
- The practice has a deeply embedded long hours culture that hasn't changed, purely because no one has questioned it. Or worse, people have questioned it and have left due to poor results.

Working longer hours does not lead to better quality work or even more work completed over a period of time. In *Deep Work*,[2] Newport describes how the company Basecamp received lots of criticism for putting its staff on a four-day week. The criticism was that staff would have to cram more into each of their four days. What actually happened was staff worked more effectively. They achieved more in less time by prioritising and cutting out the chaff.

Employers would rather keep a good employee than replace them, even more so if they become more efficient! I am not saying you should never work late; sometimes there are deadlines that come out of nowhere or you need to impress a client, but this should only happen a handful of times a year, not every evening or even every week. Why not run your own experiment like Basecamp?

CHAPTER 2

How to be an architecture student and still have a life

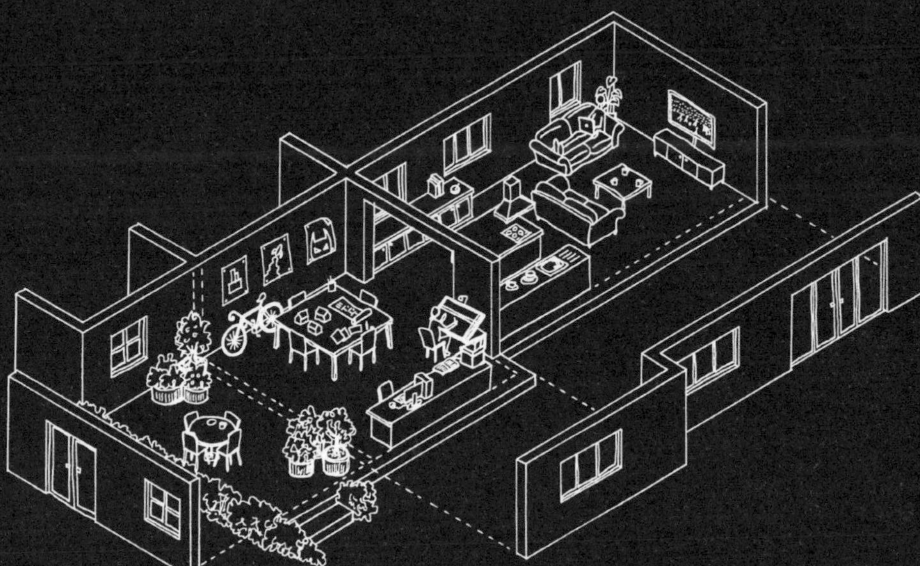

This section applies specifically to architectural students, but many of the same issues occur both in practice and in education. By my final BA year, I had discovered a way of working that did not demand long hours or high stress and that kept me healthy. I share that here, alongside observations from teaching at Oxford Brookes University.

MAKING THE MOST OF ARCHITECTURAL SCHOOL

University is a fantastic place to explore all your interests, not just your degree subject. I have described in the next chapter how I made the most of my German exchange. I also made the most of my time as a student in Cardiff, joining the triathlon club and exploring the Welsh landscape on my bicycle. I had a keen interest in sustainability and I was fortunate to have a course director, Patrick Hannay, who shared this. Today, this is a practice specialism which not only makes my colleagues and I happy at work, but also gives us something different to offer clients. Ever since my degree I have consistently read and attended conferences on eco-subjects. That is a lot of extra knowledge gained through an interest nurtured early on.

I studied Part 2 part-time while working. I didn't want to lose the useful experience I was getting, nor fall further into student debt. I embraced the opportunity to explore sustainable building workshops (usefully very hands-on!), get involved with an Architecture Sans Frontières (ASF) project at the Eden Project (see Chapter 3) and attend extra vernacular tutorials beyond what was necessary. The late Paul Oliver's vernacular lectures – part-architecture, part-anthropology – blew me away. I couldn't get enough. I spent hours poring over *The Encyclopedia of Vernacular Architecture of the World.*[1] Listen to those things that excite you. This, combined with the excellent International Regeneration course lectures by Dr Aylin Orbasli and Marcel Vellinga, sparked an interest that took me all over the world on research for my dissertation and led to a book.[2] The vernacular knowledge helped me enormously with my understanding of eco-design and made it all 'fit' into a useful offering for clients. Working

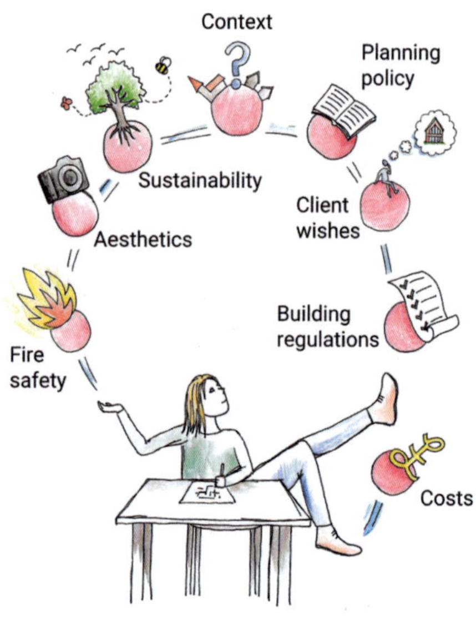

FIGURE 2.1 Drawing of an architect as a juggler

FIGURE 2.2 Vernacular studies at Oxford Brookes University led me towards design using vernacular technologies in modern housing schemes such as this one

with Melissa Kinnear and fellow students at ASF directly informed my business model. This is why it is so key to just relax and follow your interests; you never know where it will lead you. University is not all about the degree, there is so much more to experience.

As a student, I discovered that I enjoy making scruffy concept models and dislike final 'perfect' models. I am a starter of projects and don't enjoy finishing them so much. Today, I get around this by working with great finishers, who are not so keen on the things I love. I also discovered that I found 3D visualisation and CAD skills easy. However, I did not want to become a draughtsperson or a 3D visualiser. It would have bored me, and also there is so much cheap competition out there for this type of stuff, especially overseas. Instead, I used these skills to make our CAD processes more streamlined (early adoption of 3D Vectorworks, for example) and develop my own website. If you can get to the bottom of what makes you enjoy these things, it's not always about the activity at hand, rather the skills and interests that lie beneath, that enable you to do that thing well.

As you develop, you may want to specialise. The workplace values good all-rounders but also those who have something particular at which they excel. There should be no immediate pressure to find it, as the best ones are usually those that have come out of a long and winding, intriguing path to true success. If you treat life as a path of discovery, it's a lot more fun!

One of my particularly clever friends didn't pursue architecture in the end (after, it has to be said, some shockingly bad work experience), but the architecture world's loss is children's gain. At the primary school she works

FIGURE 2.3 CASA Caracol by Daniela Von Riegen of Ecosol Arquitectura, built using a leichtleim system

at, her pupils are treated to truly imaginative learning, wonderful illustrations and story-making. We need more teachers like her! Many former colleagues have set up practices together to enable work around children. One such practice combines architecture with furniture-making. Architects I stayed with in the mountains around Santiago built their own proto-type house out of a 'light-straw-clay' system *(leichtleim)*: it was then used in earthquake-proof housing in areas of Chile. The point is, you may not realise at the time, but university is a great place to sow the seeds of something that will help you later, architectural or not. Too much focus on achievements and grades may blinker you to other opportunities around you.

I am far from an artist in terms of my drawing ability. My lack of 'perfect' drawing skills could have hindered me. Instead, I use scruffy drawings to explain ideas to my colleagues and clients. I also use 3D CAD to help me quickly set up a perspective or I draw over photographs. It enables the very fast transfer of ideas, something clients love. Why waste time on an idea that hasn't got legs? Far better to have a conversation and move on to the next one! This will help you to save time on student design projects too.

WHAT DO YOU WANT?

You don't need to know immediately what kind of architect you might like to be, but do notice things that make you happy and excited or calm and content. When life gets busy, it helps to have these things to fall back on, to think, 'I used to love this, how can I bring a bit more of that back into my busy life?' It's all a learning process, but paying attention is a useful habit to start now.

In working life, you have less opportunity to explore. Simply attend a lecture because it is interesting or join a club because it sounds fun. Work out what you enjoy and pursue that; you don't need to do something because everyone else is doing so. The more you can follow your own path, the more you can stand out from the rest, either in the job market or with a business of your own later on.

Cal Newport's book, *So Good They Can't Ignore You*, debunks the myth of 'following your passion' and instead shows some rules for developing rare and valuable skills that can be used to negotiate better positions, with more control, autonomy and potential for a mission.[3] It also contains uplifting tales of successful people and their wandering career paths.

WHAT DO EMPLOYERS WANT?

As Stephen Covey says, 'start with the end in mind', and then work backwards.[4] Find out what you most enjoy, what makes you excited within or outside architecture. All our experiences build up to a unique offering that we can give the world. Don't stress too much about what that first one might be. Just follow your interest and good stuff will follow. If you follow what others are doing because it seems like the right thing to do, or may be the easiest route, you will soon become disillusioned. Be brave and find out what you want!

Good employers generally receive many CVs. Yours will stand out if you can demonstrate how your values match theirs. Employers know that well-matched employees will become an asset to their team, will always be motivated and will bring ideas of their own. It's tough for an employer to make a good decision at recruitment stage. It's costly for them to get it wrong. Make it easier by demonstrating your interest in them.

As an employer myself, I choose people who take the time to write a relevant cover email, highlighting what they like about my firm and how they feel they could fit in. I am primarily interested in their experience (not just in architecture) and attitude to life and work. It amazes me how many applicants

FIGURE 2.4 Example of a scruffy drawing

do not read the advert properly or simply don't bother to include a covering email with their CV. With 20 applicants for an architectural assistant position, I only opened the CVs where there was an enticing cover email.

WHICH SKILLS TO DEVELOP

Technology is improving at an alarming rate and some jobs that we have today will not exist in a few years' time. I mostly see this as a positive. As a junior in the office, I had to spend a lot of time putting together door schedules. For a creative, data entry like this is mind-numbing. I am very thankful that software can do this for me now. I believe that as technology takes away much of the grunt work, we will have more time to solve problems creatively, to spend time in nature (which is sorely needed to overcome the climate crisis) and to socialise. To spend more time being human, essentially.

It will take a very long time for a robot to be able to be as creative as a human being. Developing your creative and problem-solving skills will therefore make you useful in the job market for the long-term. AI and software do not have empathy or any human emotions. Jobs requiring these skills are ideally carried out by humans. Architecture requires us to understand clients and sometimes varied and multiple user groups – other humans. Robots cannot do this. Architecture requires us to solve a problem completely outside the box. Robots can't produce ideas/sketches like humans can yet, and these are areas to develop your talents – where robots and/or cheap labour cannot compete. Seth Godin, writer and marketeer, has spoken a lot about this on the Tim Ferriss podcast – worth a listen and a follow of him generally.[5]

By all means become competent and quick with software; maximise what is available. Certainly, don't get left behind. However, don't think that everything must be produced on a computer. Some of the best work (and the highest grades) I have seen were achieved by hand drawings or a computer/hand-drawn hybrid. University is a great opportunity to improve your drawing and craft/workshop skills. There is plenty of time to improve your computer skills in an office (when you will really wish you had spent more time drawing at university). Don't aim for super-high visuals; these take hours and hours to perfect and are often disappointing in comparison with a relatively quick sketch over a computer 3D printout. You will get many more marks for the communication of your ideas in sketches than in one visual. Prioritise your time accordingly – how can you make the most of your natural talents and produce a high-quality presentation in the least time? This is a fantastically useful asset for your future time-pressured working life.

Adam Grant, in Chapter 3 of his book *Originals: How Non-conformists Move the World*,[6] discusses how quantity of work is the key difference between successful creatives and non-successful ones. The successful produced a huge volume of work which contained a lot of dud ideas but also some real gems. This is a more successful approach than focusing on one 'great' idea. I would also recommend Flora Samuel's book, *Why Architects Matter.*

A CHALLENGING MARKET

In the 10 years since I set up my own practice, there has never been an 'unchallenging' year. There will always be something. Whether it affects the whole world (such as the banking crisis or Covid-19) or mainly the UK (such as Brexit or the local market around you – for example, HS2 has had both positive and negative effects on the local economy), these things are notwithstanding individual concerns. Being pregnant had a negative effect on my business. Even when you have a high level of workload, poor mental health can be a consequence or the work itself can be really tough. Clients, bosses or colleagues can cause you problems. You will undoubtedly make mistakes yourself and feel utterly terrible about it for months (this terrible feeling shortens dramatically with age and experience). Life is challenging.

Overall, these bumps give you resilience, they prepare you for even tougher challenges ahead. Two things help me to deal with challenges:

1. **Understanding economics and priorities.** People still spend money in difficult times, but their priorities change. Frivolities go out of the window and they focus on what they really need, from basic food and warmth to emotional needs, such as identity (who we want to be in the world), mental health and family. If you have an offering that is not frivolous, that people truly want and need, you will out-ride any recession. Priorities have nothing to do with personal income levels; some of my clients have been living in caravans. Understand your client's priorities and you will prosper. If you are working for a practice, this still applies to you. Which practice gives you the most in terms of learning, job security, job satisfaction and quality of life?
2. **Thinking long term.** Overall, what do you want from your life? What do you want to leave behind? This can feel too scary to think about when you are young, but a basic vision of where you would like to be in five or 10 years' time is really helpful. I now think about 25 years hence and what will happen to my practice when I retire. These long-term goals, though potentially scary, help you to understand the smallness of the current problem. Recessions end (and can be themselves fertile ground for creativity; out of constraints comes beauty, after all), Brexit will pass, even Covid-19 will be mitigated. Where do you want to be after all of that? What can you put in place now to enable small steps towards that

goal? At times, running my practice and fighting the eco-fight has felt utterly hopeless, depressing, soul destroying and unrewarding. However, these times are small in the grand scheme of things. Time and again I remind myself of my ultimate goals and that 'the world needs good eco-designers like me'. If I give up, isn't that even more depressing?

MENTAL AND PHYSICAL HEALTH

As a tutor I have noticed that due to the high grades required to enter architecture school, many students are used to excelling at everything. These students struggled the most mentally with the shift to architecture. Architecture is hard. I will repeat that in case you skipped over it. Architecture is hard. It is completely different to A levels (it doesn't exist as an A level for a start! It's a completely new subject). The practical side, in particular, combined with the endless balls that architects need to keep in the air while simultaneously designing something, is really tricky. Not only do you need to be a reasonable expert on all of those balls (building regs, sustainability, fire safety, aesthetics, context, planning policy, client wishes, costs – not an exhaustive list! See Figure 2.1), you have to know how it all comes together and the final building might be built. I don't know of any other course that combines this kind of technical/practical ability with the need for high level conceptual theory. Hanging around with too many others at architecture school, and later on in practice, can lead you into a false sense that this should be easy, because everyone else seems to be doing it. My advice is to hang around also with non-architects. You will start to understand that 90% of the population can't draw at all, let alone to the standard of visualisation required at architecture school. You will learn that they cannot understand space; they wouldn't have the foggiest how to build. They haven't a clue about sustainability. And it goes on. There will certainly be clients who might be able to manage one or two of these skills but bringing it all together is what we, as architects, do uniquely in comparison with all other professions. Never forget the value in that! Notwithstanding, there are so many other industries that benefit from these skills. It entirely depends where you want life to take you. Once you understand what a challenge studying and practising architecture is, hopefully this will help you to not feel like a failure, as we all do at times. Like many things, studying architecture is a process. Keep putting one foot in front of the other and you will get through it.

Here are a few tips to help you to maintain good health throughout your studies. The previous chapter also deals with mindset and pressure, plus there are time-management systems in Chapter 8, which you may also find helpful. Finally, I would wholeheartedly recommend Dr Emma Hepburn's

Instagram feed.[7] She is a former architecture student who switched to psychology and produces lovely drawings about mental health.

Establish a routine

When you start at university, for the first time in your life you will be in charge of your own schedule. This can feel liberating but also very intimidating. I found it helpful that my university insisted we attend the studio every day from 9am to 5pm. It was a great discipline and enabled lots of social interaction and help from our peers. It developed a studio culture that we loved. Today, with more pressure on university space, some universities cannot provide a studio space that is available most of the time. There can be huge gaps between lectures and tutorials, and those gaps can be daunting to fill productively. The temptation is to avoid work and chat with friends or procrastinate online (under the heading of 'research'). I would highly recommend reading Cal Newport's book, *Deep Work*, on how to split up time effectively into 'Deep' and 'Shallow' work. There's some very interesting research about how creatives benefit from structure and also how the author managed to get high grades by only working until lunchtime each day. He filled the rest of his days with social activities or hobbies. I personally group my work into categories and timetable them into a weekly schedule. That way, I am not starting each day not knowing what I should be doing. The Stephen Covey scheduling practice (detailed in his book[8]) is a fantastic tool for maintaining good mental health because it identifies personal development and you as an individual as a separate role, meaning that you don't forget to include space in your week for that important time.

Sharing Food

Sharing food with friends is such a heart-warming human activity. It's very nurturing when living away from family and a great way to keep each other healthy and energised for your work.

Exercise

It can be so easy to get into a panic-fuelled sleep/work cycle, with unhealthy snacks to keep you going. Our bodies are not machines. Sooner or later this kind of cycle will break you, whether mentally or physically. Being ill does not help you achieve your deadlines, so pace yourself! Regular breaks for exercise are proven to increase productivity (especially in nature – Newport[9] describes how a walk in nature improves concentration). The mental health benefits are enormous too. You might not enjoy exercise for its own sake, but university is a fantastic place to try lots of different things. You may well find something you love, setting up a great habit for life. Not only this, but also the rhythmic action of exercise has been shown to improve creativity. Countless times I have dragged myself away from my computer, gone for a walk and come back with an idea that has saved me vast amounts of time. It's hard to pull yourself away, but it really pays to do so!

Regular social contact

Many famous artists and writers have enjoyed the coffee house culture where they could share ideas and perspectives with others. These regular breaks inspired them and motivated them to produce great work. Just a single coffee with a friend can lift the spirits enormously and is one of the huge benefits of university life – embrace it!

Get perspective

I like looking at the stars or the sea. When you look at something that vast it makes you feel small and therefore so does your problem (see Chapter 1).

Don't let others sway you – 'their work is so much better than mine' – it's very hard to see the brilliance of your own work. Peer pressure doesn't go away, so it's worth accepting and dealing with it now.

Don't do all-nighters

I did this once. It was a massive waste of time. Really think about when you do your best work. I bet it's not between 2am and 9am. It's more likely to be between 10am and 1pm or perhaps 4pm to midnight. Young people's body clocks are different. There is lots of research to suggest that getting up early does not suit young people.[10] Everyone is different. There are early birds and night owls and inbetweeners – find your best time and you will breeze through work that is much harder at other times of the day. Make the most of this time consistently and you will work far less hard, be far less stressed and get much more sleep (and social time) outside your study commitments. Don't get sucked into working later and later; the quality of your work will slip, and you will become more paranoid and isolated. A very talented student of mine nearly had a nervous breakdown caused by working nocturnally. Humans need daylight. You don't need a mental problem on top of your workload. You need to finish the course, enjoy the course and have time for a life outside of it. That takes a bit of discipline to organise but you will reap the rewards and have time to enjoy being young!

When I was a student, I found starting work at 9.30am or 10am suited me really well. I worked until a late lunch and then had a long break, which included some form of exercise. I would often re-start work around 4pm or 5pm and work until 8pm or 10pm. I had plenty of sleep and good breaks and plenty of social opportunity. I maintained that throughout my final year and felt really well throughout.

CHAPTER 3

Background

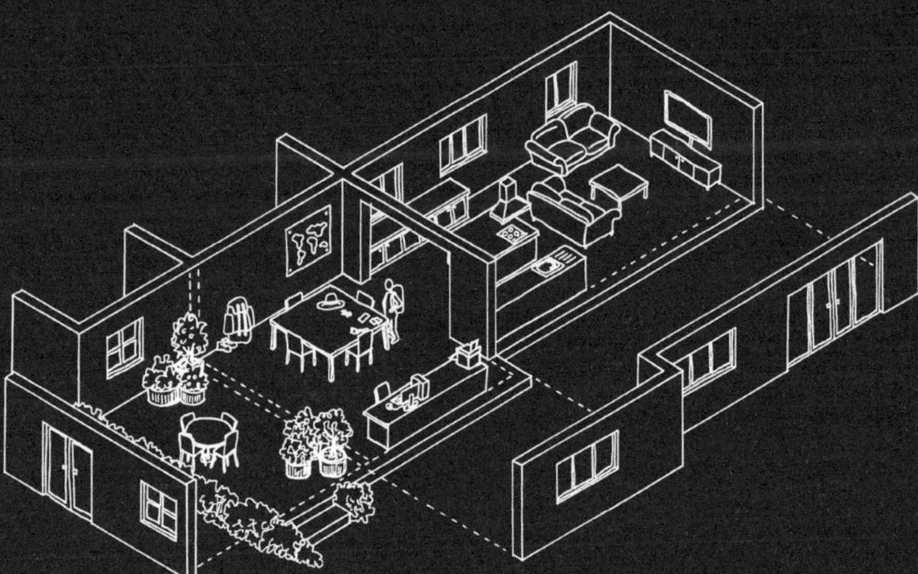

WHY ARCHITECTURE IS AN INTERESTING CAREER AND WHY I ENJOY IT

When I was five years old, I remember looking out of the window on a rainy day and thinking, 'Whatever I do with my life, I don't want to be bored.' There aren't many careers that offer as much variety as architecture: there is huge scope to broaden your horizons and also to find your niche, as I have done with barns and eco-design. As well as types of architecture project, there are also different types of architect you can become, such as a business owner – like me – or a technical design expert, a Passivhaus consultant, a cutting-edge designer or a head of creative re-use projects or skyscraper projects within a large firm. You can specialise in landscape, interiors, exhibitions. The list is endless. The Royal Institute of British Architects (RIBA) is well respected abroad, so if you are an RIBA Chartered Architect, opportunities aren't limited to the UK either.

Through buildings, architects have the ability to improve people's lives in a significant way. The job can be stressful, but it never stops being challenging. I am certainly never bored.

WHAT LED ME INTO ARCHITECTURE

I originally wanted to be a racing mechanic for a Formula 1 team. After a week's work experience for a Formula 3 team at Silverstone racing circuit and further research into the profession, I discovered there was not enough design involved and I needed to do something more creative. I thought of architecture (partly due to my dad's training as a chartered surveyor before returning to farming and later converting barns) and spent a day with a family friend who had an architecture practice. I should mention that I would never have dreamt of entering the engineering world if it hadn't been for a turnaround at secondary school, where, thanks to an inspirational maths teacher (thank you, Mr Peterkin) I changed from 'someone who is not very good at maths' (primary school assumption) to 'someone who is good at maths' (and loves algebra). Good teachers are so important.

My second inspiration came from my art teacher, Mr Childs, a former architect. It was he who suggested I should take an art and design foundation course, to decide which area of design I was most interested in pursuing. I was desperate to go travelling, but begrudgingly went to the college interview anyway. I was given an unconditional offer of a place, which surprised me. Perhaps, I thought, it would be a good idea to spend a gap year exploring design instead of travelling.

I loved my foundation year; being in the workshop, making items of furniture, and I particularly loved working with metal and welding. As a result, I eventually decided on Interior Architecture as my undergraduate degree. My primary interest was creating space, and I felt that a seven-year architecture course was a bit too daunting, especially considering that my A level results were not great.

I chose Cardiff (University of Wales Institute, now Cardiff Metropolitan University) because I had a good feeling about the tutors and the place. The tutors seemed kind, passionate and not at all aloof. Cardiff is a relatively small city. It has the sea and the hills on its doorstep, it seemed full of opportunity and at the same time friendly and disinhibited. That degree was to become the best Interior Architecture course in the country at the time. It was here that my interest in eco-design was realised and supported by the course leader. He fed me books and told me that the world needs good eco-designers. This advice never left me, but it was hard to negotiate such a position when I began working in architects' offices. Only since 2019 and Greta Thunberg has eco-design become more expected and more prominent.

Living in Germany

In my second year at university, I lost my way a bit and an Erasmus exchange to Germany was probably well-timed. I found the course in Germany had a much heavier construction bias and so I took the opportunity to improve in this area. I went with a friend from university and we both struggled with the language for three months. At the end of the exchange, I had made a huge leap in language ability and was suddenly able to hold a basic conversation. I was amazed that this was possible and intoxicated by the thrill of learning another language. These new skills gave me courage. Presenting work to your peers in another language is surprisingly liberating, rather than scary. There's an invisible barrier between you and your words. I wanted to communicate my ideas and that over-rode any anxiety about public speaking. Having sweated and stuttered my way through presentations in the UK, I was a different person on my return. Additionally, the understanding of nuance and body language is heightened when you don't understand every word. This is very useful in building client relationships and weeding out potential problematic ones before signing a contract. When travelling in German-speaking countries, I feel very confident. I can understand what is going on around me, it makes me braver, but also safer, and I stick out less because I am not nervous. Likewise, in South America my Spanish enabled me to travel to isolated places and not worry.

My friend and I decided to defer our next year at university and to continue living and working in Germany. The Hochschule Mainz allowed us to continue studying there, if we paid the fee (€120 a semester, which included a free bus pass – an amazing deal, especially compared to the £3,000 a year university fees at home at the time). The German education system in 2003 was very relaxed and it was possible to be a student for as long as eight years and pick and choose your modules. We chose modules that we felt would improve our portfolios. I managed to get a part-time job in an Italian coffee bar. I ran the tiny 'Stehcafe' (a stand-up café) myself, taking the money to the bank at the end of the day. Talking with customers quickly improved my German and I became very self-reliant and organised. If you run a café alone, you have to make sure you have everything prepared, as you have no one to run an errand while you look after the shop or to help when it's busy. I loved not having a boss looking over my shoulder, resting legitimately (not needing to pretend to be busy) when it was quiet and working hard when it was busy. I also taught business English to individuals and small groups on a self-employed basis, which was quite lucrative. I took the opportunity to learn Italian, Spanish and French. The cost of living in Germany at the time was very low and I found it quite easy to live from my part-time earnings. In many ways, I had a higher quality of life there than I did in the UK with a full-time salary. Interior Architecture is a well-known sector on the continent. Towards the end of my time in Germany, I managed to find some work experience at an Interior Architecture practice, which opened my eyes to formal office German as well as the different architectural office culture. I also learned about team dynamics and roles in a micro practice. The lifestyle seemed to be fantastic, which was very inspiring. I understood design could be well rewarded financially and could provide a nice quality of life outside work.

I returned to Cardiff, finished my degree and embarked on a three-month placement in the architecture department at the University of Liechtenstein in Vaduz. Following this, I began working again in UK architectural practice.

MY ROUTE TO ARCHITECTURE

My professional career started at a small firm specialising in one-off country houses and planning expertise. Architects were mainly employed there just to work on design and planning applications. However, I wanted to learn more about construction and to work on bigger projects, so I moved to a larger firm.

It was around this time that I applied for an ARB Part 1 exemption. I felt that my Interior Architecture BA was limiting. In the UK, at that time, it suggested a preference for interior design. Many presume Interior Architecture is all about cushions and curtains. In fact, it is more like a specialisation in spatial design and refurbishment (a predominant project type in most architectural practices). It is frustrating that the UK has not caught up with European attitudes in this area.

Initially, I found the new, larger practice unfriendly and stressful, and I felt unsupported. I sat in a windowless corner: it was dark, either too hot or too cold, always stuffy and very unsociable. There was also no indication that this was an architect's office: no models, no drawings on the wall, no sign of creative activity at all. Later, the practice moved to a self-designed office on the fourth floor of the same building. This had large amounts of glazing: openable windows! We could see the sky! The temperature was easily managed and because of this, we rarely used the air conditioning in summer. The office atmosphere vastly improved following the move; we were more sociable and I felt much happier about coming to work. This all led me to realise how important physical surroundings are for happy, productive work.

Despite difficult beginnings, I found my feet and really flourished at technical design stages. I pushed eco-design on every project, learning how to persuade clients of the benefits. I even achieved a lower energy police station! I found site visits exciting and inspiring, but also scary. There was a huge gap in my knowledge of how buildings were actually put together. Despite this, I developed a good relationship with builders, as I was always happy to help and to learn. However, it wasn't always easy. In one instance, I disliked being shouted and sworn at over the phone by a developer client and told him so. At this point I was still a junior in the very open-plan office and everyone was surprised at my confidence, but after this we developed a good working relationship. The lesson I learnt is how important it is to set up good boundaries from the beginning.

Part 1 Exemption and benefits of Part 2 part-time study

In June 2006, I decided to go ahead with obtaining an ARB Part 1 Exemption. It was an exhausting and time-consuming experience to put together a strong portfolio for the exam. It is also very expensive and there was always the possibility that I might go all the way to London to find I had not even got as far as an interview, losing the £1,000 fee in the process. I also spoke to the practice I worked for about potentially working part-time to study the Part 2 Diploma at Oxford Brookes University, which it was happy to allow. I received my ARB Part 1 Architecture Exemption in August 2007 and started Part 2 at Oxford Brookes in the September of the same year. During term time I worked 24 hours a week and in holidays 35 hours a week. I found this suited me very well, as I had just about enough money to live on and it gave me one day at university and one day to study at home. Inevitably, I studied through most of my weekends and evenings, which could be exhausting, but I thoroughly enjoyed the course, even though things like my triathlon training suffered. I discovered my own limits!

It was while studying Part 2 part-time that I realised a few useful truths.

It did not matter that I was out of the office two days a week while I was studying, despite running three jobs on site (ranging between £1m and £5m in size). This dispelled the myth that you can only be a full-time architect, in the office, five days a week. This was because I communicated my days in the office to the contractor, who then only contacted me in an emergency out of hours (this only happened once, that I can recall). I checked my work email once a day while at university, in case of any emergency. I could then ask someone in the office to sort out the problem or at least gather more information to help me on my return.

On the day of study that I had to myself, I was my own free agent. On these days I would achieve stacks of work with no distractions and still have time to exercise and cook a lovely dinner. I didn't want this flexible lifestyle to end.

Other alternative routes: Apprenticeship and the RIBA Studio

It is great that an architectural apprenticeship has finally come about. This route would certainly have attracted me. We need a variety of architects from all kinds of different backgrounds and the apprenticeship helps open architecture to those for whom the traditional route would not work. Fear of academia, debt or university costs should not be the reasons that people choose other careers.

I regularly examine on the RIBA Studio course (not an apprenticeship), the only one of its type in the country, run at Oxford Brookes University. It requires only two or three examination presentations a year, meaning that students can study from anywhere, all the while maintaining their experience in an office environment. It is just like a traditional architecture course with modules to complete, but students hire their own private tutor (usually from a local university). They also assign themselves an office mentor from their practice. Practices can financially support students if they choose, but it can also be self-funded. It is tough, but students enjoy it, many of whom have families to support.

EXPERIENCES FORMING MY BUSINESS MODEL

Discovering my 'team model'

It was while studying my Part 2 at Oxford Brookes that the opportunity came up to work with ASF at an outdoor classroom at the Eden Project. We were a small team of five, all Part 2 students with different skills. I enjoyed the collaboration with the others and how our strengths naturally came to the fore. This project was slotted in around studying and, for me, work in practice. I learnt that maximising team strengths was also excellent for time management. We mostly worked remotely, coming together for accountability and to share ideas and make models. I enjoyed the autonomy of this way of working, and we still learnt a huge amount from each other and had a lot of fun.

This planted the seeds in my mind of how a team could operate effectively in a way that utilised everyone's strengths and allowed lots of flexibility. Without realising it, I had discovered my 'team model'.

Travel with a purpose

In 2010, amid the recession and shortly after the prime minister made education funding cuts, the practice I worked in started making redundancies. After the third round, they asked if anyone would like to take six months off (for a sabbatical, a baby or otherwise), hoping things would have improved by the time they returned. Having submitted my master's dissertation proposal prior to finishing Part 2 at Oxford Brookes, I realised this would probably be my only opportunity to embark on six months' travel to carry out the necessary research. I knew I was taking a big risk. Not least because my boyfriend (now husband) and I were saving for a house deposit, my half of which I would need to spend on the trip. However, I had wanted to complete a round-the-world trip since I was small and here was a good excuse for travel with a purpose (the best kind). It would also give me an opportunity to emulate the late Paul Oliver

FIGURE 3.2 El Bolsón, WWOOFing in Patagonian Argentina. 'La Casita', a hand-built, tiny house I stayed in, is made from recycled pallets filled with recycled glass bottles and straw, and is clad in a milk, mud, clay and horse manure render.

(who lectured me at Oxford Brookes), whom I had admired so much for his architectural and anthropological studies overseas. The title of my masters' dissertation, 'Can vernacular technologies be used in a modern day context to create sustainable housing design, one that represents climate, culture and environment?' would later form the basis of my first book.

I bought a plane ticket with my savings and organised WWOOFing (World Wide Opportunities on Organic Farms) and couchsurfing to keep costs down. Despite the minimal cost, the value of these experiences was enormous. I learnt how people really live in different countries, giving me empathy and an understanding of different cultures – useful as a designer. It improved my Spanish enough to be able to interview Bolivians without a translator. It would not have been better if I had spent more money. This mindset helped me to be creative with start-up funding and building experiences. I was pleased to receive free accommodation and food in Papua New Guinea in exchange for my research about the mining relocation housing project. This taught me the value of independent research. As an outsider I could speak frankly with the residents and gain new understanding. I learnt how similar humans are across the world, with the same worries, and I learnt a great deal about the importance of home, cultural beliefs and status. All these apply to UK home design and helped me to understand the market back home. It took me several months to organise all the various meetings and interviews around the world, as well as other practicalities and visas. There were some nail-biting moments in

FIGURE 3.3 Interviewees on Mali Island, Papua New Guinea.

the preparation. During the trip itself, the Chinese professor I needed to interview suddenly disappeared to the other side of China! A lady I was couchsurfing with in Xi'an helped me find and interview an alternative professor. People love to help. This applies equally to architecture and business networks I have in the UK.

Despite losing my job later and the loss of savings and income (and therefore the long delay until we could buy a house, by which time house prices had risen again considerably), I do not regret my sabbatical at all. It opened my eyes to so many different cultures, completely different from my own. I met some fascinating people and, because I travelled alone, was able to get close to understanding what it is really like to live in the countries I visited. It gave me a huge sense of achievement and independence. It proved that being a bit brave could bring huge rewards.

FIGURE 3.4 Lijiashan, China. Outside the cave dwellings I stayed in.

Jobless

In April 2011, when I returned, the county was still in a full-blown recession. I lost my job, as my projects had been passed on to others while I was away. I was easy to lose. I applied to about 100 architectural practices, to no avail. Previously, sending my CV to five practices would get me three job interviews. I applied for multiple admin/reception/office type jobs but was always told I was 'over-qualified', despite many of those roles being temporary. This was frustrating, as while a student I found it very easy to land temporary office work in the summer. In the end, I was forced to sign on at the job centre, a horrible and demeaning experience that did not help me find work and reduced my confidence significantly. I have huge amounts of sympathy for those who suddenly find themselves homeless. If it were not for my family, I could have easily found myself there too.

CHAPTER 4

Going solo

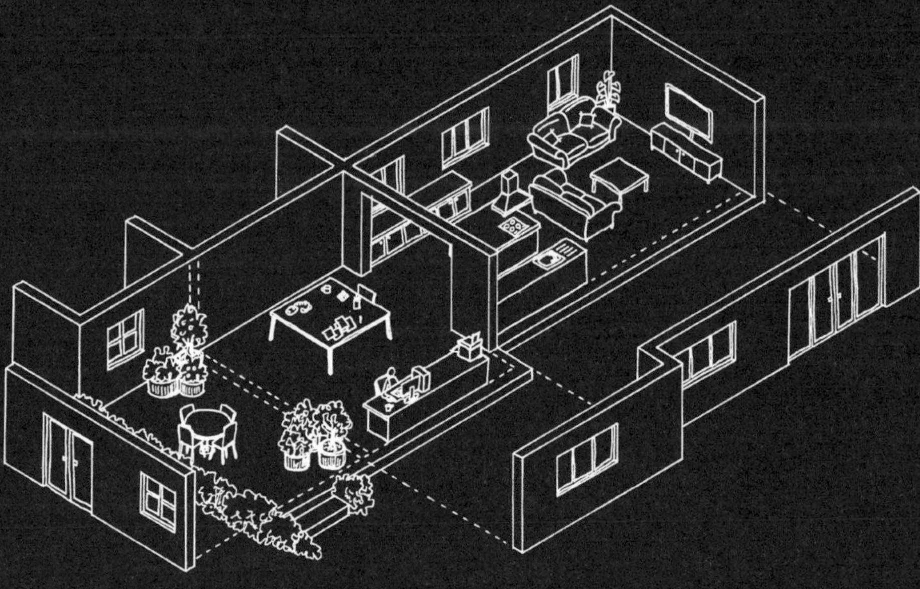

FIGURE 4.1 The author working from home

THE BEGINNING

Freelancing

Two months after redundancy, I was fortunate to bump into an architectural designer who had offered me work in the past. He still needed help, so I began working for him on a freelance basis. This was when I was first introduced to Vectorworks, which provided me with huge efficiencies later when I started my own practice. It was also useful to work on interesting contemporary domestic projects; a complete change to the schools/prisons/healthcare projects on which I had previously worked. This, and other freelance work I did during this period, gave me some insight into how different types of building projects are managed.

Unfortunately, I found working remotely during this period very stressful. It seemed to be the worst of both worlds. I didn't feel in charge of my time at all. I had to drop everything to complete work in two or three days, with very short notice of work coming in. Plus, I had no employee benefits. I felt isolated and unsure of the quality of work I was providing, especially as I had very little prior experience of working on domestic projects.

During this time I received interest from friends who wanted extensions, but I was wary of taking out Professional Indemnity insurance, which must be continued for six years after project completion. In reality, the lowest insurance bracket (£250,000 for architects) was very affordable, paid monthly, and should not have presented such a barrier.

Start-up from zero (or minus) and first client

Eventually, I began to see that this freelance work was unsustainable, and the job market was not improving. Although I have always enjoyed coming up with business ideas and thought I would someday set up with a partner, I would never have been brave enough to have launched Clare Nash Architecture (CNA) when I did. The job market gave me the push I needed. I was 29 and had very little experience of the residential architectural market. I also had only six years of working in architectural practice under my belt. Additionally, most new practices start with at least one client and some kind of business plan. I had neither, but I could see that setting up my own firm would be beneficial if I wanted a family later, and overseeing my own time again was very appealing.

So, as has often happened to me in the past, I made a decision based on gut instinct, switched my mindset, bought insurance and started advertising on a budget (postcards in local shops, cafés and estate agents). I got a lovely job as a dinner lady (serving school meals in primary schools for a local farm shop with a sideline in catering) and cycled the 6 miles there every day to save money on petrol. This small income really helped to keep us afloat while I got started on the architectural projects in the remaining time. I enjoyed being a dinner lady very much and was well looked after by the business owners (sadly, all too often this kind of respect is unusual when working in minimum wage jobs). Yes, if big bills came in, we were sunk, but it was an otherwise good existence.

Architecture requires very little in start-up costs. This was fortunate because I was fresh from redundancy and in a small amount of debt. I set up with just a new laptop and a decent camera (from my studies). Initially I couldn't even justify a laser measure (they have since dropped in price considerably), so I outsourced to a surveying firm.

My first client was my husband's friend (an eco-extension project). Once I had decided to set up on my own, I thought I ought to tell people that I was an architect, so I started doing this at social events. It felt awkward at first, but most people are genuinely interested to find out what you do. I still had very little experience in domestic work, so I read lots of magazines to find out more about legislation, costs and opportunities. In those early days of CNA, designing took much longer and I earned very little.

Main fears and how I overcame them

Because I had very little experience of domestic architecture, I feared not being good enough for my client's aspirations and set low fees in accordance with my self-esteem. As an extra challenge, I was also trying to push an eco-agenda. Working on Passivhaus detailing was stressful and scary. I learnt as much as I could from books, blogs and from attending conferences. I also

FIGURE 4.2 CNA's first self-build: a low energy home and testing of Passivhaus design principles in Northamptonshire

received help from Passivhaus experts. Although daunting, there is nothing like a real-life project to give you the push you need to step up. I learnt a huge deal on my first project and the final outcome for the client was fantastic. Finally, by working for myself, I was able to put my ideals into practice.

In the very early days conferences were unaffordable, but by attending my first AECB (Association for Environment Conscious Building) conference as a speaker, my attendance was free! By carefully picking the right kind of conferences, I was able to build my eco-network and learn a great deal from other industry specialists.

Having recently studied Part 3 in 2009/10, the multiple ways in which an architect can get caught out and potentially sued for negligence was still very fresh in my mind. In fact, I still worry about this. It is completely normal. I console myself with the fact that most people are adults and are not out to get you. My concerns just make me a more conscientious architect. After all, my primary fear is a disappointed client. Due to this, I have consistently worked on improvements to our systems and customer service. I am doing my best and that has to be good enough.

THE SHIFT FROM ARCHITECT TO ENTREPRENEUR

Legal structures define businesses as sole trader, partnership, LLP or limited company, but there are much finer nuances than that. Freelancers are set up as sole traders. Freelancers can have more freedom and flexibility than those in salaried roles, but essentially they are still swapping time for money, just as you swap a salary for time spent working. There is nothing wrong with this; mostly this is the fall-out of lack of flexible working practices within the industry. This should change exponentially post-Covid-19 because working from home has shown practices how flexible working can be beneficial. However, at some point you need to make a decision. Do you want to operate a business or do you want a job with more freedom?

If you want to run a business, you need to have a plan for the next five, 10 and 25 years. It's important to know where you are heading so that you can steer the ship. You will likely need to aim for a profit that is in addition to your salary (to enable future investment and the potential sale of the business). For example, I want to create a legacy whereby my business has enabled great leaps forward in terms of eco-design in the face of the climate crisis. I want my business to continue beyond my lifetime, run by other eco-aware architects. In this way I am not just exchanging time for money: my business is about creating a movement and change. Businesses come in all shapes and sizes. Having one does not mean that you need to build a team, have a lot of people on payroll or work on certain project types. There are so many variables and possibilities. I cover more on this at the end of Chapter 5.

I find it helpful to make goals for the year that, just like the Stephen Covey method (see Chapter 2), cover all your roles. For example, my business goals for 2020 included spending more time in the countryside and swimming and taking small steps to enable a move back to a village.

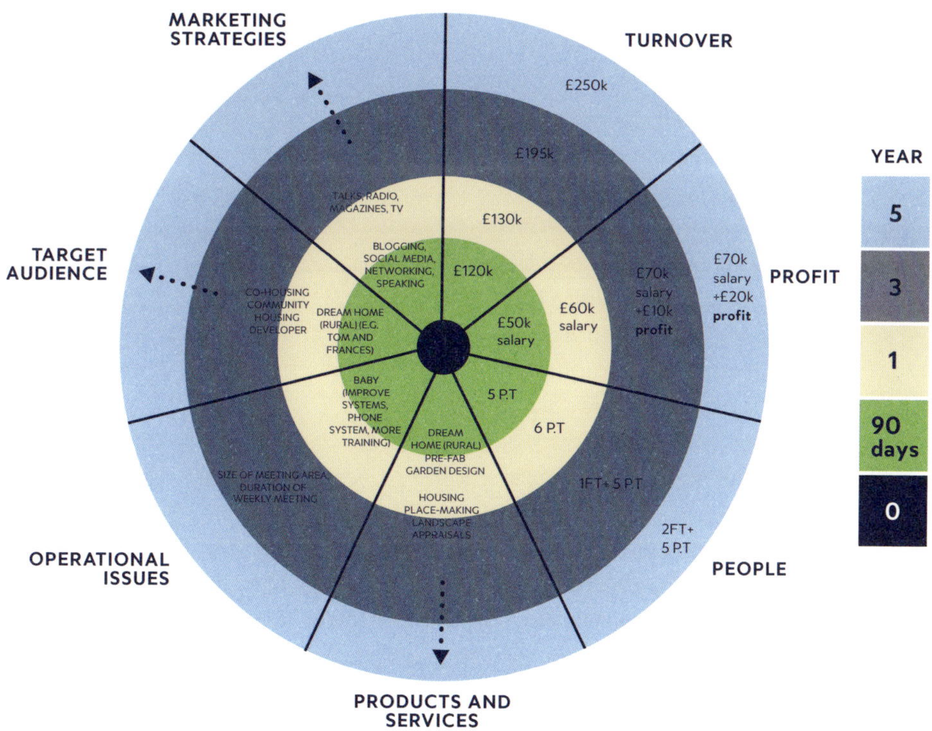

FIGURE 4.3 Example of a Five-Year Plan vision

Because I set these intentions for the year, looking back on 2020 I can see how I did spend more time swimming, more time on my allotment (in the countryside) and I allocated money for finishing house projects to enable a move next year. I also increased my personal income by a third, worked on more eco-projects and I wrote this book. All goals that I set for myself in January. When I set goals, I use the SMART[1] technique. It's a useful prompt and ensures you don't get away with vague plans. I add these goals to my accountability software to keep them in mind throughout the year.

THE MANY DIFFERENT HATS OF A SOLO ENTREPRENEUR

This chapter covers all the 'hats' of an architecture business. There is more detail about how I have used systems, processes and outsourcing, as well as employee strengths, to ensure I am not a stressed-out juggler. I also use my own strengths to maximum benefit, delegating my weaknesses.

One of the biggest challenges with setting up as a small firm in any kind of business is that all at once you must wear all the hats: admin, sales, marketing, finance, etc. It's not enough to simply be good at what your firm does, you also need to know how to run it successfully. I felt hopelessly under-educated in this area, especially on the finance side. With very little money, I resorted to second-hand business books and the library, as well as business blogs and podcasts. There were also some free local business courses, designed to increase rural business support in the area. I discovered The Business of Architecture by Enoch Sears, an American architect challenging traditional architectural practice in terms of sales and marketing. Later that year I also discovered entrearchitect.com, another American architect running a small residential architecture firm that in the last few years has gone from

FIGURE 4.4 Balancing all the hats can be tricky

owning a successful office in the US to working from home, with the rest of the team on a remote working basis. Sears first educated me about the importance of a niche and a target audience. I established this further with knowledge gleaned at networking events and from a marketing consultant who wrote a strategy for me to follow. The strongest outcome from this was the success of targeted blogs. These brought in not only more work but also our favourite kind of client (eco-aware).

It is important at the outset to think of all of the hats as separate jobs. I doubted very much that I would need employees at the beginning and therefore found it quite difficult to separate out roles for my new team. I was doing all of them, so each one simply blurred into another. It was not very efficient and it was very distracting to be in charge of so many things. As they say, 'Jack of all trades, master of none'. If I was setting up a firm from scratch now, I would write systems for all of these roles as I was creating them. I would also split my time into 'roles' from the beginning, helping to define them for future delegation.

Finance

Initially I did all the bookkeeping and tax returns myself. This was very simple to do and very easy when any mobile phone can take photos of receipts (I use the Scannable app, which directly links to Evernote, a note-taking app). To save money in the beginning, I think it is a good idea to do this part yourself (unless you are hopelessly unorganised or cannot set up a simple spreadsheet), as it saves quite a bit of cash initially and gives you a good understanding of how the system works. Later, it made no sense for me to waste my time working on these things. I did not train as a bookkeeper or an accountant and clearly it was much better for business if I spent time working on architectural projects, winning work or working on the future of the business. I now use Xero (an online accounting system) in combination with an accountant and bookkeeper. Even prior to using a bookkeeper, Xero saved me so much time and hassle; a massive improvement on my spreadsheet.

The best and most transformative thing I started doing in 2013 (should have been much sooner!) was to set up and use a cash-flow forecast. There is more about this in Chapter 8.

Marketing and networking

In Christmas 2013, I built a new website on WordPress. It took me around 40 hours (a lot of which was spent deciding on a theme to tweak on Theme Forest(!)) and it made all the difference.

I really enjoyed creating it myself and this was quite easy to do in WordPress. I think architects are naturally quite good at graphics and presentation design. They also don't require an e-commerce website or

FIGURE 4.5 Photos such as this one helped me to find my niche in barn conversions

anything complicated to begin with. So, plenty of cash can be saved here by doing it yourself.

After a problematic oversight in 2017 (see Chapter 7), I now use a website man for technical help and maintenance. I used to do this myself but working with an expert enables me to try more exciting things, takes the stress of maintenance away and he brings a lot of good design ideas. 90% of our work comes via the website – it's important.

I cover more about developing a niche and marketing in Chapter 6.

Poor salaries of solo practitioners

If you read any of the salary surveys, you will likely be disappointed by the salaries received by sole practitioners. There are many reasons for this. Many sole practitioners are female and are working part-time around family. They have left a mainstream job due to a lack of part-time opportunities. They are not necessarily business-minded, they just need flexible hours. I have already mentioned my lack of self-esteem on the launch of my business. This led to very low fees. It wasn't helped by there being so little published on the matter. Perception is also crucial. Whenever I put a fee together, it seemed like an enormous amount of money, as I was judging it entirely through my own lens. At the time I was struggling financially, so I was used to being very thrifty. I judged clients' depth of pockets against my own. This is a wrong way to think about it on two counts:

1. You cannot possibly know the financial situation of a client. I have had clients living in caravans whose first priority is a self-build and they could afford my fees. However, a professional with a much higher income would often prioritise a new car instead.
2. You should always price on value to the client, not your time or your perception of what is too much/too little.

It took me a long time to understand the true value of my work. I am still working on it now. It will evolve as my clients' needs evolve. I had a big awakening when a developer client of mine made £200,000 profit from a tiny architectural fee. However, it isn't just about financial value. Living in a beautiful, healthy home is priceless for many people. As long as the works and your fees stack up with the sale value, the client will understand the benefit.

Another reason that sole traders' salaries are so low is that they are often competing with architectural technologists or technicians for domestic work. Architects' fees seem high in comparison to theirs. You therefore have two options: either you sink your fees to match theirs (as many do) or you demonstrate the added value that you provide in comparison. You cannot expect the client to understand from the outset. I have lost count of how often architects have bemoaned the lack of client understanding. It is our job to explain the value of an architect to clients. They haven't attended a school of architecture.

It helps to look at it from their perspective. When have you personally questioned the price of a service, and why? Probably because the value wasn't made clear to you or you simply didn't need it that much. You had other priorities. When clients are buying architecture, they are buying a lifestyle. They want to see themselves in your past projects and imagine their new life with what you can design for them. This is what you are offering that is different to someone cheaper: the ability to deliver the

FIGS 4.6, 4.7, 4.8 AND 4.9 Clients want to imagine the lifestyle you will provide them with

lifestyle they want. A list of qualifications or services does not deliver that. Just as I discovered on my travels, our homes are all about our perceived status. In the UK there are different ways of displaying this – a fancy new kitchen space to show off to friends, a large new country pad, a super-slick and high-tech extension or a natural eco-home. Just like other things we buy, they represent how we see ourselves.

Some sole traders say that the saving they are making on travel and overheads means they don't need such a high salary for a great lifestyle. I fell into this trap, too. Eventually you just get sick of such low reward for such high responsibility.

FUTURE-PROOFING YOUR BUSINESS

Also, relevant here is the skills section in Chapter 2, which talks about the necessary creativity and human factor of architects compared with robots and AI. The pandemic and recessions have taught us that nothing stays the same forever. At some point, as a small or large business, it will be necessary to make changes. This might be due to disrupters in your market, a new architect moving into the area and offering something competitive or a global recession. During the Covid-19 pandemic it could have meant working on more domestic projects than you do usually because people were stuck at home during lockdown and commercial office projects had dried-up due to working from home. The important thing is to keep your eyes open, spot changes early and be prepared to adapt. Some changes are temporary and fill a gap; others can be more long-lasting. Knowing which of these it is helps with planning and investment. Mostly I have found these big shifts to have been ripe for opportunity. I carried out fascinating research abroad and set up my own business during the 2008 recession. In the Covid-19 pandemic I advertised garden design, which was popular and good fun to work on in lockdown. It would have been easy to drop my fees and work on the multiple small kitchen and home office extensions that were in high demand, but I knew this would send me back to juggling too many projects and potentially a loss of money. I believed that the pandemic was temporary, the climate crisis was not going away and therefore neither were clients wanting eco-design. It made sense to pursue garden design, as this ties in with my overall aims for the business. The lesson here is not to pivot for its own sake – make it relevant to your own values and goals. That way, even if it doesn't work out as you hoped, it will still have taken you further along the right path.

CHAPTER 5

Team

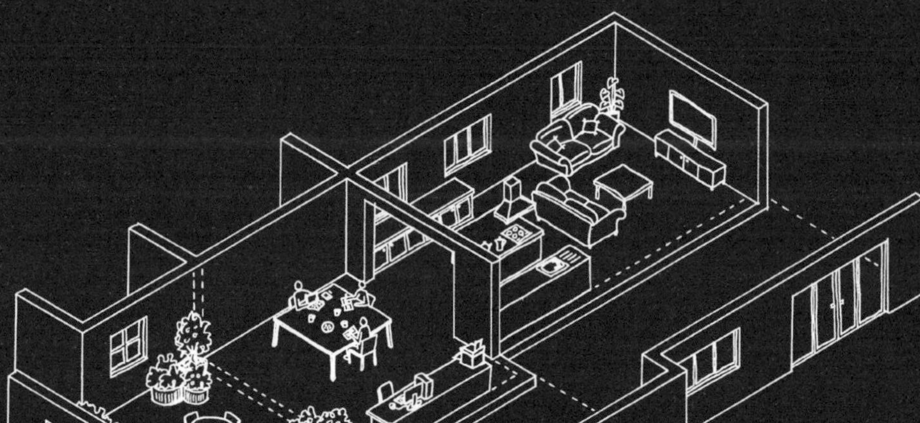

FIGURE 5.1 Illustration of the CNA team as it was in 2019

When I decided to employ staff at CNA for the first time, I wanted to challenge the long hours cultural norm in architecture and give hope and inspiration to students entering the workplace. I am fortunate that through teaching I had access to a large pool of student talent at Oxford Brookes University.

FIRST EMPLOYEE AND TRAINING SYSTEMS

This was a hard step. I feared taking on a team. I was worried I would not be a good boss, that people would find the work boring, that I would not be a good leader. I have always felt comfortable working as part of a team but not being in the spotlight. Previously I had thought I was happy working on my own. I didn't want the concern of employees (nor the paperwork, which turned out to be a doddle compared with my expectations) but I soon realised that I was never going to escape the relentless drawing work or have any time to focus on progressing the business (a previous strength) if I didn't employ. Initial team meetings put me in the spotlight, as my employees were expecting me to lead the meeting and to organise projects on which they could work. It felt quite intense. This was a new role for me. However, meetings quickly became much less about me and much more about the work we were doing together. My colleagues regularly tell me how much they look forward to meetings, so clearly I had nothing to worry about! Another concern was about losing control of projects. The reality was hugely liberating. It gave me the freedom to progress the business, use more of my strengths to improve project delivery and focus on bringing in more exciting work – all because I was spending less time sitting at the computer drawing.

Working with freelance staff is, of course, another option. I decided against this because I had previously had a lonely and quite stressful time as a freelancer, and I wanted my new team to feel supported. I wanted to invest in them and pay them employee benefits. I also realised that if I was targeting students, they would be unlikely to want to set themselves up with HMRC, as they would eventually seek a full-time job on completion of their course.

I used my contacts at Oxford Brookes to circulate a job advert and soon found myself with three Part 2 students to interview. I chose Lucy, who seemed bright and ambitious and had worked on conservation projects. She told me straightaway that she would be looking for work overseas once her course had finished (around six months' time) and I thought this would be a good opportunity to test out having an employee without a long-term commitment. I felt extremely awkward at first – giving instructions was new to me – but Lucy soon freed up my time enough to see the light at the end of the tunnel.

Things I learnt from my first employee:

- I realised that you don't need a perfect 'finished' business before you take on employees, but it really helps if you have some systems in place that they can start using quickly. This reduces your time training them and increases their confidence.
- Ad hoc in-person meetings (around one a month) are just not enough. There is such a thing as working too remotely. I changed this to a weekly meeting with the next two employees. This has worked really well for the past seven years.

Just prior to Lucy leaving for Australia, I prepared by putting up an advert at Oxford Brookes Jobshop (free!) and by using tutor contacts to distribute the adverts to their current Part 2 students. Non-teachers can contact tutors using LinkedIn to find them. People outside a university can still advertise on their 'jobshops'. Other successful methods I have used have been sending out a job description by email to those in a trusted architectural or business network. Other practices have successfully used social media. I advertised two positions – for marketing/book administration and for an architectural assistant. I itemised the jobs they would be doing so that the advert would attract people who would really be interested in working for me. There is a lot about me and my ethos on my website, so I included a link to that. I received a good number of applicants, and for the interview I especially chose people who had taken the time to write a relevant cover email, highlighting what they liked about my firm and how they felt they would fit in. I barely looked at their grades. I was only interested in their experience (not just in architecture) and attitude to life and work. All the four interviewees were highly capable, but I felt that the two I chose initially had such interesting experience (one with a self-initiated trip to Bolivia and good on-site experience; the other with experience working for a German practice).

Having read Michael Gerber's *The E-Myth Revisited: Why most small businesses don't work and what to do about it*, I knew the importance of creating systems. To create these systems, I wrote Evernotes (a note-taking app similar to One Note – you can organise notes, keep website articles, scan in drawings) with screenshot how-to aids, including 'how to set up drawings', 'what to name drawings' and how to complete certain tasks in Vectorworks. Every question I received from then on was turned into an Evernote and we now have a useful library to refer to using common language. One of the issues with googling software queries is not knowing the right terminology to gain the right answer to your problem. I also created drawing standards, standard filenames, etc.

Expectations

Initially (and due to such a young team), I retained all the client communication. With 20 jobs to run, it was tricky keeping up with it all, but this was still less work for me than before. By handing over easier tasks to the team, I was able to answer more email queries. Today, each of my team members run projects, including client communication.

At the time of employing staff, I was only a five-year qualified architect. It was still fresh in my mind how it feels to be a Part 2 student and working at the same time. You're very keen not to make mistakes, but you also have plenty of energy for new challenges. Personally, I have always struggled with 'not being good enough' or imposter syndrome. This was quite acute when I was a junior in the office. Every mistake I made was taken personally and further proof that I wasn't good enough. Because of this, I was keen for my employees to feel very supported and not to have the finger pointed at them for mistakes – because everyone makes them, it's how we learn!

This is one of the reasons that I would finish off drawings that had been started by others. It meant that I saved time on the setting up of drawings and I didn't need to report back on everything that was missed. Gradually my colleagues picked up more and more of the differences between what they had produced and what the finished article should look like. Quite soon, I was merely marking on edits that they could make themselves.

These days, I do very little drawing work. I tend to produce quite a lot of scruffy sketches to explain my ideas and leave it to my colleagues to work out the remaining design and the details. Initially I was very hesitant about doing this. I had worked for a technologist who would show a client an attractive sketch at the initial meeting. The rest of the team would struggle to make it work and receive none of the glory. Occasionally the sketch idea didn't work at all and again the team took the flack. As more of an introverted designer, I prefer the slow cooker approach. Although I will often give ideas to clients verbally on the spot (from my library of previous work), I rarely sketch with them. I feel intimidated by people watching me sketch and find my best ideas come when working alone and intensely. I read and re-read the brief. I look at their chosen images, I sketch and ideas ping through my brain. In the end, having a baby forced me to focus on just doing those sketches and very little further drawing work. I realised that this, together with marketing, winning work and problem-solving, were the most important jobs for me to perform, both for the practice and my team. When working out your own strengths, self-awareness is key. Various personality tests have helped me, but they aren't for everyone. Noticing when time flies and work feels easy, as opposed to when you feel drained, are key indicators of strength areas and weak areas. You have to work harder on a weakness, which is why it is draining, even if you or others perceive you to be good at it. I personally disliked being micro-managed by others, so have naturally given team members a lot of free reign. However, with good briefs and weekly checking-in sessions, it's simple to catch things before they go on a tangent. It is important to retain the company ethos when delegating, whilst accepting some loss of control (which is enormously liberating by the way!). I do this by employing staff with the same values, by engaging them in the company vision and by brainstorming new business directions or ideas with them. We do this weekly but also at our annual bigger team coaching sessions run by Maggie Newton. If the team understands the full history, it's far easier to make good decisions.

Today, most of the firm's projects are not run by me but they receive a lot of my input at office meetings and on Slack. It's all a team effort. Because we are all working using our strengths, we are better together than the sum of our parts. Working alone, I would have less time to use my strengths and it would be much harder and more exhausting to reach the same level of output.

TEAM WORKING AND THE OFFICE MEETING

The weekly meeting is fundamental to how the CNA business model works. I learnt from experience that freelance work can be isolating and stressful. The team meeting is crucial to ensuring staff do not feel unsupported.

FIGURE 5.2 One of our office meetings in 2016

WHY NO OFFICE?

Through freelance work, working with ASF and part-time study, I discovered that I enjoyed the autonomy over my own time that working for yourself gives you, notwithstanding the opportunity for other activities, such as teaching, writing and research abroad. I worked out that due to being out on site and teaching, I would only be able to sit in said office for two full days a week. I couldn't see the point of getting in extra work just to pay for an office with a view of a car park. At home, I have a view of my garden and chickens, which I prefer. As an introvert, I also really enjoy the quiet time to do focused and enjoyable work. Lastly, no commute and flexible hours means I have more time for my hobbies, such as swimming and my allotment. It also means that the office is more environmentally friendly – we still use a car to travel to site, but we don't need to go to the office first or afterwards, so that is a big saving on mileage.

It is an agile, flexible and more efficient model. We can respond quickly to trends, political pressures, a recession, new business directions. We don't need to bring in work just to keep the business going; instead we choose work that is aligned with the firm's mission, where we want to be in five years' time and what we all enjoy working on. Without the financial tie of an office, our biggest overhead is software. As well as considerably reducing the pressure to take on work, the whole team also works more efficiently without the distractions of a busy workplace, saving time on projects. Every employee also saves on travel time and cost to get to work.

How does it work?

So down to the nitty-gritty of how a non-office model operates. Staff use their own laptops; the company provides the software. Staff upload their hours each month to Xero Projects. Our VA collects expenses and sends them to my accountant. Staff mainly work from home, but the business pays for them to use a local co-working space when they need a change. This is still far cheaper than office rent.

Communication is key for this remote working model to work. Slack, a business communication platform, is preferred for team communication when working remotely. We regularly meet clients on site in addition to the weekly meeting, but for convenience the latter sometimes happens in the nearest pub or café to site. Mostly we use the Crisis Café in Oxford and I enjoy that my office fund is supporting homeless people in gaining skills. Our meeting is hugely inspirational. It is not just a resources meeting, we design co-housing schemes together, we discuss site problems, design issues, the state of the world. We come to these meetings full of energy because we have spent the rest of the week apart. Although I am the director, we all have a go at everything, staff are heavily involved in business direction, discovering new efficiencies, new ways of doing things. However, we do play to individual strengths.

I have been asked whether this non-office model will need to change as we grow. I don't think it will need to change much. We might plan some work-together days instead of just meetings. This would also help with training new staff. One of the key aspects of this way of working is its agility. I would be keen to retain that and not enter into a long-term office contract. The CNA mindset is to remain flexible and open to change; whether that's the business structure or employee contracts or type of work, it's important not to get stuck in a rut.

It doesn't suit everybody and other drawbacks of the non-office model

Some people thrive on the energy of being in an office all day. So this model isn't for everyone. I am very clear about our non-office model in job descriptions, so it's a choice from the outset. We get many speculative applications to work with us because we operate differently. Personally, I prefer bursts of collaboration spaced out by quiet time for deep work and thought. This model suits introverts but extroverts can also enjoy the flexibility of a variety of activities, such as networking, and can also choose to work in a co-working space. Practices could certainly offer more options so that employees can choose.

You do need good cloud-based systems and good internet.

You lose the ritual of going to the office, so you need to replace this with something else – a different kind of morning routine (see Chapter 9).

Staff skills: communication is key. It does take guts to ask questions when you are stuck, but it's possibly less frightening than doing that in an open plan office when everyone can hear you. Team members must be happy to work alone or use a co-working space.

FLEXIBLE AND PART-TIME WORKING

You don't need to be office-less or work remotely to achieve many of the benefits of our non-office model. Much of it comes down to flexible working. As long as the whole team comes together for core office hours and collaboration time, the rest could be a lot more flexible than a standard 9am to 5pm. Using a ROWE (Results Only Working Environment) means staff can be measured by the results they produce rather than hours sitting on a chair. This is much more efficient! Benefits that we enjoy, such as:

- staff retention due to flexibility and autonomy
- more focused 'alone' time working away from distractions
- less wasted time commuting

could all be achieved with a flexible working model. It doesn't stop there. We all enjoy the advantage of off-peak gym and cinema, lower cost childcare and quieter roads. In winter you can go for a two-hour bike ride in daylight. Weekly meetings are more fun and intense; we don't get bored with each other. Commuting less is better for the environment and we can support local businesses. We are a mixture of larks and owls and in-betweens at CNA. Flexible working allows us to work at our most efficient times, making work feel easier.

Many people, not just women, have caring responsibilities. Paying for care is expensive and can mean that people are forced out of architectural work to avoid these costs. Flexible working, remote working and part-time options can enable those with caring responsibilities to continue developing in a field they love. Practices can only benefit from a more flexible mindset. Many of the practices in Chapter 10 operate a flexible and part-time working policy. It also allows for variety. Many at Transition by Design (TbD, see Chapter 10, Case Study 4) pursue other projects, whether that is charity work, research or teaching. This also provides safety in difficult times, as diversifying your income stream can make you extremely agile.

Taking it a step further to a remote working model (as many did during Covid-19) means you can work from anywhere. We have all enjoyed working from abroad or different parts of the UK with extended family.

It is possible to be a part-time architect, which can be very refreshing and balancing, especially on demanding jobs. My experience as a part-time student, as a business owner with a newborn and as an architect with other 'jobs', teaching and writing books, proves that you don't need to be full-time on projects; clients cope.

The client expectation that we need to be available to them and full-time on their project is a false one. Most of our clients are busy professionals or business owners juggling projects of their own. They get it. If you are a full-time architect, it's rare that you would be working solely on any one project, therefore your time is split. It makes no difference if you are unavailable because you are busy on another project, in a meeting or if you are at home looking after children. The experience for the client is the same. Projects at CNA are shared, we have good systems for handover and it's easy when one of us is away for any reason. The directors at Harrison Stringfellow Architects have job-shared successfully for years (see Chapter 10, Case Study 2). We have never had a client problem that came about due to one of us working part-time.

If you are attracted by going office-less or using a shared space instead, feel reassured that clients no longer need to see an office to take you seriously. The website acts as an office showcase today.

Despite designing a part-time role aimed at Part 2 students to fit around their studies, two of my employees deliberately sought out other part-time architectural work once they graduated so that they could remain working at CNA. One has told me that she enjoys the flexibility (she can go for a swim in the afternoon), she applauds that everyone is paid for every hour they work (there is no unpaid overtime) and she really enjoys our weekly brainstorming/designing/debating meetings. I have found this model retains excellent staff who I really don't want to lose.

As explained previously, when taking on students I thought it best to employ them, but wanted to offer them more hours in the summer and time off for final submissions. The easiest way to do this was with a variable hours contract. Staff fill in timesheets and they are paid for each hour they work. This suited all my employees (who have thus far opted not to change to a fixed salary) who had other commitments (either study, research or other paid work). However, I expect it to change to fixed salaries for some team members in the near future. There are downsides to a variable hours contract – for an employee it can mean fluctuating income. As an employer, it is riskier because staff are not obligated to fixed hours. There needs to be trust and discussion on both sides and regular re-appraisal to ensure it is still suitable.

I believe that we are not getting the best out of people by demanding they work 9 to 5 in a city office every day (or much longer in architectural firms). People are not necessarily efficient between those hours, as there are night owls and early birds. Working from home during the pandemic has given many employees an opportunity to trial a more efficient working pattern. Hopefully, managers will be able to see the benefits and it will be allowed to continue post-pandemic. As humans we have good and bad days. Some days we are really involved in a project and will gladly work until 10pm on it; other days we would rather have a break, go for a walk, have some thinking time. Offices that demand a person sit at a desk between certain hours are not using people efficiently. Allowing that break, that thinking time, ensures people produce better quality work and are motivated. With more sleep and time for other activities, people make more intelligent decisions. When my VA had a baby, her working hours changed to when the baby was sleeping. Our flexible system allowed her to do this. With childcare at such a high cost, this offers a much better lifestyle without reducing income. Later, when I had my own child, I too found this flexible system enormously helpful.

In order to make this work, you have to trust people. Presenteeism cannot exist. I have never understood the lack of trust in architectural staff. We have trained for seven years because we want to do great work. Why not trust us with flexible hours? I was amazed when an otherwise very proactive office I used to work for (which has since changed its policy) did not allow a returning mother to work three days a week. As a part-time Part 2 student, I was working three days a week and studying for two. You might say 'well that's OK for junior staff', but I was running three large commercial jobs on site simultaneously. It was never an issue with the builders or the client, as I managed my time and communicated effectively. Working without presenteeism means that your work is entirely judged by its quality and timeliness. This is called ROWE or Results Only Work Environment. I have observed in myself and others how being in front of a desk does not mean you are productive.

Post-lockdown, many firms have recognised this. Previous reasons to not allow flexible working – such as you needing to be always available for effective collaboration – have been totally disproved. It has taken a global pandemic for people to make this work. Of course, there have been issues, but for many it has been a huge positive.

Choosing team members

One of the many benefits of team working is useful input from others. It is always useful to have a different perspective and another pair of eyes. It is important to employ people who share your values but who are better than

FIGURE 5.3 Team photo in 2019. Katie (second from right) now works at TbD

you in some areas. Otherwise, you will always be limited. I struggled to hand over logo design to a qualified graphic designer, but once I had done so, the result far exceeded my expectations.

Initially, I chose my new colleagues based on their experience, attitude and eagerness to work with me. Since then, we have used DiSC and the Talent Dynamics personality tests to work out our strengths and weaknesses. The Talent Dynamics wheel was most useful for identifying job roles within the team; DiSC has been helpful for understanding ourselves a bit better, as well as client types.

For someone like me (a creative, ideas, project-starting type), I need people skills and detail as my support team. Personality tests can make it easier to see who you need to fill those gaps.

Prior to discovering these tests, I had intuitively created my ideal support team in the form of Katie, who has great people skills and is good at supporting and organising others. My husband is good at detail. Julia is a more detail-oriented version of me. Soon after, I met Rebecca, a VA, who became an excellent client first contact with strong people skills.

Personality tests are very helpful for loosely identifying what you need and gaps to fill. However, be wary of putting people in boxes. As we develop and grow, we naturally move into other personality types. This could simply be exposure to different work, highlighting a new strength. Especially as a young architect, you are developing all the time. In a large office, I was known as the 'building-regs queen' for some time. I relished the practical side of architecture, but as a junior I wasn't given that much opportunity to use my creative skills. These came out much later. As did my more extroverted side, which suffered a lot with lack of confidence. These personality tests help to identify team weaknesses, which you can either fill through recruitment or help to counter with training or mentoring. Having identified a team weakness for technical and detail design, I wrote a job advert requesting someone with a keen interest in that area. I didn't know about Talent Dynamics then, but I was looking for someone in the Winter/Steel spectrum. Jaina didn't take a test until later, but this is exactly where she fits. She is now our chief systems orchestrator! Last year, Katie left the team to work with the inspirational co-operative TbD. We have definitely noticed the gap that she left. I now need a bit more extroverted style support to keep me motivated, so I often work with a coach (Maggie Newton) in this category.

Introvert/Extrovert

For some reason, our society values extroverts more. They are the loudest in meetings, the quickest to speak and can seem like the most creative sparks. If you are introverted or have an introverted partner/spouse, it is worth reading books by Susan Cain about the benefits of introverts and societal extrovert bias. I am half-and-half or an Ambivert.

When we have completed personality tests as a team, those who find themselves more in the introverted spectrum or without creativity as a strength sometimes feel that they are less talented or perhaps boring. 'Gosh, that makes me boring doesn't it?!' is a common outcry. This logic comes only from societal pressure. It is wholly untrue. Introverted people are responsible for some of the most highly intelligent and creative endeavours the world has ever seen (Albert Einstein, J.K. Rowling, Meryl Streep, Mahatma Gandhi, Barack Obama, Bill Gates and Elon Musk, to name very few). We just need to create a society in which these skills are valued more and allowed to shine.

Architect or manager or partner/director?

Whether you are a business owner or an architect working for others, as your career progresses at some point you will find yourself making a choice between being an architect or a manager/business owner. This can be a tricky transition. As a Part 2/Part 3 architect in an office, I found myself wondering why anyone would want to become an associate, as it seemed to mostly involve managing others. At that time, I loved being a project architect, mostly managing only myself. However, things change. I didn't choose the role of team leader, it was a necessary consequence of taking on employees. Although project management is not a strength, I enjoy collaborating. However, being a manager in an office, being asked questions all day, would drive me potty. So, I have created the kind of business model that suits my leadership type. Even within an office environment, it was well

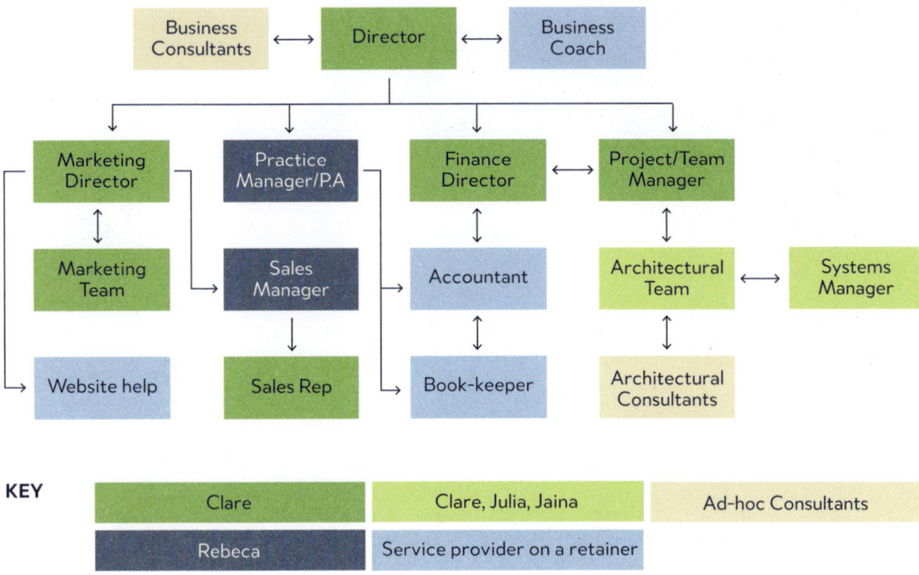

FIGURE 5.4 Who wears which hat now

known that I disliked interruption. You don't have to conform if it stresses you out! People will still enjoy working with you, more so if you are happier.

Within architect partnerships, you will often find a more outgoing type paired with a more introverted type. This is ideal, because with the same level of experience you can make excellent decisions and cover for each other when you are away. With naturally different strengths you will complement rather than compete.

Many business books talk about moving away from being a technician (read architect) and becoming a business owner. This suits some people. You don't need an MBA to be a good business owner, but learning about business via books, blogs, podcasts, networking and seminars is essential. However, not everyone wants to be a business owner. If you want to stay working mostly as a project architect, you can engage another who is good at the business side of things, be that marketing, finance, project management or just admin. It all helps! Once you understand yourself, it makes it much easier to fill those gaps and accept you need help to get to the next level.

I used to wear all of these hats (see diagram below) as a sole practitioner. Naturally, some of them got missed more often than I would like! I am still wearing some hats that are not my strengths, namely project and finance manager. These will be outsourced further in coming years.

FIGURE 5.5 Projects such as this would be a lot harder without collaborating with others

The female perspective

I now work a 25-hour week but this has not diminished the level of challenge I receive from my work. Working part-time is often viewed as an unofficial demotion. Those fortunate to gain flexible or part-time hours are often disappointed to find that they are suddenly overlooked for more exciting work. I don't understand this logic from companies that only the day-to-day boring work should be given to part-time workers, those who have the potential to think very creatively. Enjoying more variety gives you lateral thinking time, space away from the core work to think differently with a new perspective. Someone I met in Santiago told me that ants have more variety in their daily work than humans do. Something needs to change here.

It tends to be mostly women that provide the majority of childcare and therefore work fewer hours. I don't think it is purely my flexible working policy that has attracted so many women to work with me, but I think it helps. In general, I find that all my colleagues – male and female, with and without children – enjoy flexible working. Many people have different caring responsibilities. Initially I enjoyed it to fit around my triathlon training and travel. This is not an exclusively female activity!

OTHER METHODS OF GROWTH

Building a team is not the only method of growth. Invisible Studio (see Chapter 10, Case Study 3) is run by Piers Taylor alone. He collaborates with others on bigger projects, as and when he needs to. Many architects decide to stay as a sole trader for the majority of their career. I know many women like this in my local RIBA women architects' group. They use our network for support to ask business and architectural questions. Another possibility is to outsource and work with freelancers. Like collaboration, this provides a lot of freedom and no commitment to salaries ongoing. This can be useful during uncertain times and in a recession.

For example, you could:

- outsource much of the admin (as I do) to a VA or an in-house, part-time PA/administrator
- have a bookkeeper and an accountant
- focus on design and planning and then work with a freelance technician to get building control drawings completed, after which you could run it on site
- easily outsource website building and management, copywriting for blogs, even the whole marketing strategy and implementation to others
- have a very wide pool of people to choose from, as technology enables virtual meetings.

FIGURE 5.6 Drawings like this are what CNA is all about – barn, ecology, landscape, context. Employing people with the same values as your own provides a wider scope for creativity within the CNA vision

For the best gains, it is important to understand where your time is best spent. Prioritising the things you are good at will be key to improvements and growth.

If you are interested in growing while staying solo or small, then Paul Jarvis's *Company of One* could be helpful. I do think there is something to be said for deciding how big you would like your practice to become from the outset. Larger practice systems are far easier to set up in the beginning, as are software choices. I have personally never been interested in creating a large practice. I like working on smaller, niche, bespoke projects with a small team that feels a bit like a family. I felt a bit anonymous working in larger practice, though the projects were exciting and experience-building.

Overall, building a team of any kind is very rewarding. I would recommend it to anyone.

CHAPTER 6
Niche and marketing

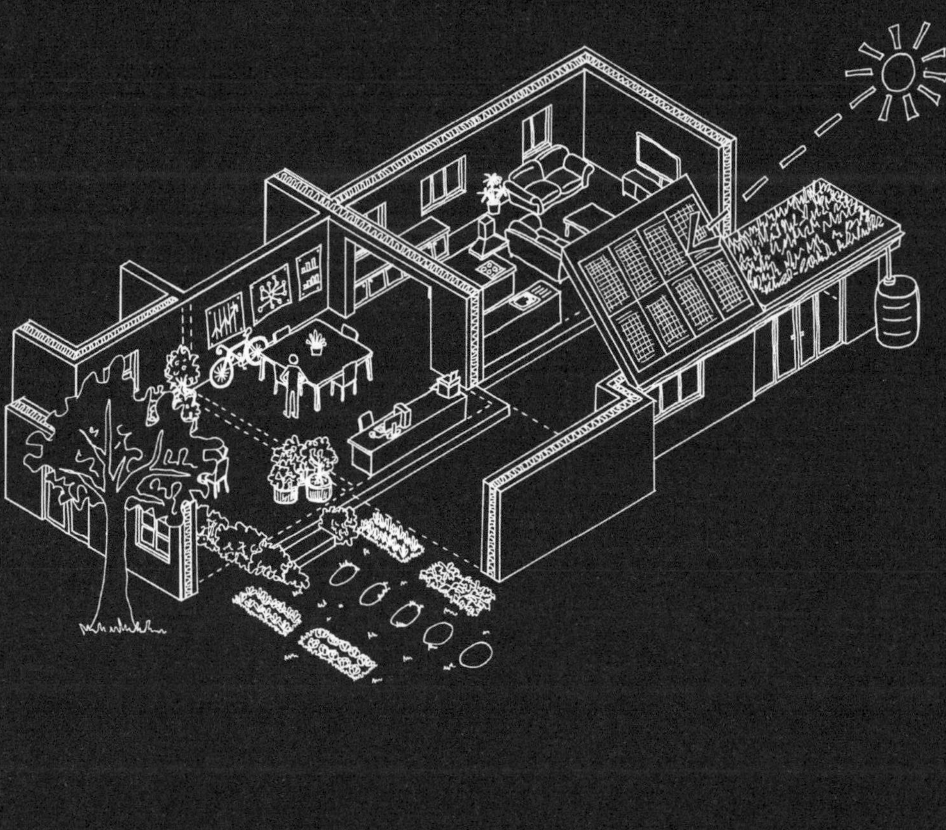

FIGURE 6.1 Photos of you doing your thing in your niche can attract clients to your website

THE ENORMOUS BENEFITS OF A NICHE/SPECIALISM – THE STORY OF MY NICHE AND HOW TO FIND YOURS

As explained in Chapter 4, I built a new website around Christmas 2013. I am a forward-thinking architect with a lot of technical know-how, but my old website was seriously underselling my skills.

Although I enjoyed the process of designing a website, it is a new skill to learn and not for everyone. I wasn't especially busy at that time of the year; I didn't yet have a child. I had time to explore something new and make mistakes.

In these early stages, I didn't have a lot of work to showcase and hardly anything was finished enough to take photos of it. Instead, I drew sketches and showed design drawings. I showed work under construction. I began writing blogs and articles about my architectural interests. The aim was to show a human to the world, because people buy from people. The main point of a website is to entice someone in and encourage them to find out more by making contact. It's important that the website represents you and your values, otherwise you will waste a lot of time visiting unsuitable clients. Likewise, misrepresentation would disappoint a client. Being authentic is key.

It's very scary putting yourself out there for the first time. You feel like the whole world is going to judge you. Despite having a blog for many years now, nothing bad has happened! However, many fantastic things have happened – mostly winning work that we are really excited about.

To get yourself out there, you first have to get over yourself. If you can understand the basic premise that no one really cares about you, then you can get braver with what you are saying. People only view what you are saying through their own lens. Take note of your thoughts when viewing marketing material from others; you will notice it's all about your own world view and how you see yourself. Big brands really tap into that.

If you are struggling to get started with marketing, I would strongly recommend working with a business coach. They can get to the root cause of what is holding you back, as well as helping you to define what you want. This makes is far easier to make a plan of action, because you have clarity. They can also help you to be brave!

Apple is often cited for good reason, because it is an excellent example of how people buy into a lifestyle, not just a computer. Apple attracts forward-thinking, creative types who see themselves as alternative. I have a MacBook and fit into that category completely (although I cringe a bit at 'alternative', as I recognise my own cliché). However, it needs to stack up practically too – a MacBook gives me huge firepower and very little interruption for my creative projects. It feels wonderful to use. Apple's customer service is superb. I will most likely remain loyal for life. What lifestyle are your clients buying into?

Knowing all of this (having studied many books and blogs on the subject) and researching other brands, I began to see how I could create my own 'lifestyle choice' for clients. After all, a piece of architecture is extremely long-lasting. It is a long-term lifestyle choice.

From my research I discovered that the most successful brands are those that have developed a niche for themselves. I started to think about what mine could be. I have always had a keen interest in eco-design but knew that alone could frighten off some clients and probably wouldn't get me enough work to begin with. I knew I wanted to specialise in something rural. My master's research into vernacular was very recent and I felt I knew how to design in the countryside. There were more personal benefits too: I would happily spend most of my working life in a field if I could! My dad was quite entrepreneurial and started converting barns before there was a fashion for it. Subsequently, I had lived through construction of three different barn conversions. These experiences were unique to me and I felt I could build on them to create a niche.

I set about writing blogs that provided the sort of information potential barn conversion clients would be looking for. Around the same time, I gained planning permission for a barn conversion as a skills swap for a friend. I used this experience as a case study and my friend's mother in-law (a skilled amateur photographer) took fantastic pictures of me 'at work' to use on my website.

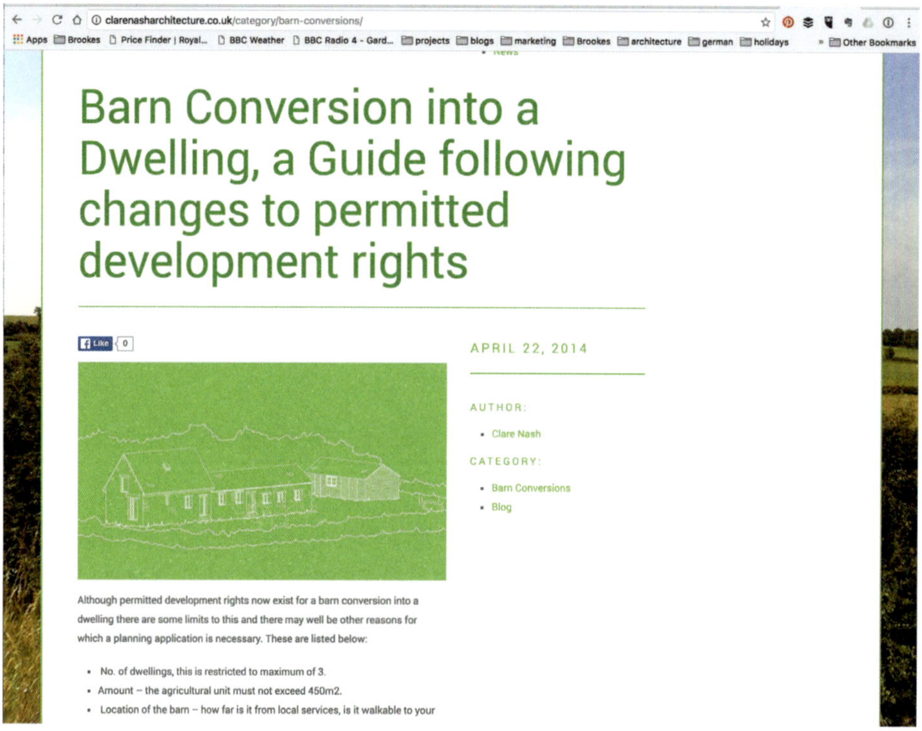

FIGURE 6.2 An example of a blog that attracts barn conversion clients

This wasn't the first time I had done work for free. I also helped a friend with gaining listed building consent and building control approval for a change of use to a café. She happily posed in photos that I then used on my website to promote my work. I learnt a lot from both these projects and the learning and the promotional material I gained set up my business to win more lucrative work in the future. I don't normally recommend working for free, but where there is mutual gain and respect on both sides, it can really help get your leg up in the early days.

Back to blogging. One of those blogs I wrote in 2014 about converting a barn is still one of my highest-ranking pages today. It took me an hour to write, probably another hour to put photos and present it well on my website, as well as checking SEO (Search Engine Optimisation). Those were two very productive hours.

Working on barn conversions and writing about them gave me access to more work in the countryside. Comfortable that this was bringing in enough work, I started writing more and more about the eco-extensions and refurbishments on which I was working. This attracted a new type of client as well as providing the icing on the cake for existing barn conversion clients. I didn't realise, until I started promoting my eco-skills, how much of an interest people would have. It's so important to test the market!

There are still people who are put off by it. I have had clients say that they aren't particularly eco but have an open mind and would we still consider the idea? I think that through friendly, not too technical blogging, I am helping to break down the barrier between eco-culture and mainstream culture. It isn't frightening, it doesn't need to cost a huge amount and it can work on all building types. Getting that message across is still a work in progress.

To find your own niche, it's helpful to work with someone else who knows you well. Ask them what they think are your top skills. It's useful to ask clients for feedback too. Think about your life and what you have learnt so far: write it all down or do a spider diagram. You should start to see some connections. It doesn't matter if you are starting from the beginning. Remember, I had never worked on a barn conversion before doing my first one. I learnt how to do house extensions from magazines. Everyone has to start somewhere.

I have consistently found that the more honest and vulnerable you are, the more appealing you are to clients. I don't mean that you should air all your mistakes like dirty laundry – clients want to feel safe working with you – but stories are wonderful ways of expressing how you tried something, it didn't work at first, but this is what did, and look at the result! Clients love that kind of honesty. It helps to look at other brands and see what you like about them. Take that insight and put it into your own marketing.

Becoming an expert – reduce your competition

Imagine you are a client looking for someone to help them with a project. Let's say it's for a café. They will type 'café architect' into Google and they will look at local architects' websites to see if they design cafés. If there is one of those architects who (a) shows up under a Google search for 'café architect' and (b) shows a range of cafés on their website and perhaps also offers interior design for said café, that's a big happy, safe decision for a client. However, if they only find case studies of a wide range of projects, they will need to hunt to find a project like theirs (very time-consuming and boring). They will likely get put off and go elsewhere. Clients are not looking to view your portfolio, they couldn't care less about the work you do unless it directly relates to the work they want doing. The more you can get into a client mindset when planning your own website, the more decent project work will come your way.

It helps to think about how you shop. Most often you will choose a specialist over a generalist if you are looking for quality. If you wanted

FIGURES 6.3 AND 6.4 Case study – before and after pictures are helpful

to improve your racing times as a cyclist, would you buy a bicycle from a generic bike shop or from a specialist supplier? Clients want to feel safe with their expensive building project. The client knows they are buying your experience and expertise in this particular area. This means you can charge more compared to the competition. You are providing more safety and likely more speed, as it will take you less time than a generalist to complete the work.

When searching on Google, clients have a specific project in mind. They will use search terms relating to that project and will be inspired by photos of projects that make them think, 'That's it! That's what I want my house to be like!' They will also value any information written in a way they understand, that helps to make the process of building their dream home seem easier. I know this, because this is what I am looking for on Google when searching for a business service or product. The more helpful the advice, the more likely I am to buy from that website, as I will have built up a trust and will feel looked after. I will also have seen examples of their work or product and found them desirable. I am not looking for a list of services or awards or accolades. I just want to see what I could be getting if I bought from here. As a first-time mother, I found thenappylady.co.uk a really good example of a niche product-based website. It even offers a bespoke nappy list tailored for you – amazingly helpful for a new mum. What is stopping an architect's website from being as helpful to a new domestic client? Nothing at all. Only a bit of thought and identifying clients' pain and your solutions to it. As a new mum, my particular pain was negotiating the minefield of cloth nappies available on the market. How to choose? For a domestic client we discovered the main pain points were:

- Can we actually afford what we want?
- Can we get planning permission on this site, in this conservation area, on this listed barn?
- We don't know any builders – how do we know they won't run off with our money, not achieve our deadlines, cause us to overspend?

What are your ideal clients' pain points?

As an aside, don't get into the trap of charging less because it takes you less time. More speed is very profitable and helpful for the client; that means you should charge more, not less. It isn't about your time, it's about their gain.

Avoid making price the only differentiator between you and other architects or, worse, those less qualified than you. I do not mean write a list of reasons why you are a great architect. The client doesn't care. They want to see a list of gains to them. They want to feel like you understand them and what they really want (which might not be what they present with). If you don't educate the client on what they gain by working with you compared to another architect, they will only be able to compare you on price, because what else is there? Offer something different and interesting and they will see the benefit.

If you want to take this even further, you need to develop an ideal client or 'avatar'. Get to know everything about them and understand what their key concerns are, then talk about them. Listen to what existing clients are telling you. What are they afraid of? What does this project mean to them? Perhaps it's quality time with their children, maybe it's a status thing, maybe they want to leave a legacy. There are so many differentials here – find yours!

Competing with others in the industry who are too cheap

Offer something wholly more valuable to the client. Piers Taylor talks a lot about this in Chapter 10, Case Study 3. What a client values will attract them to working with different architects. For example, Alexander Ilg, who runs Sägezahn architecture in Germany, is very attractive to clients because he is a carpenter and architect. He uses his own apprentices to build low-energy homes for clients. He also has a talent for saving clients' money, often by showing them how to improve quality in a smaller space. That is valuable to certain clients and not so valuable to others. What is your icing on the cake?

Competing with Disrupters

We can understand the term 'disrupter' from the tech world, where (quite frequently, it seems) new apps come out changing how we view what is possible, effectively 'disrupting' the status quo and offering more value than the competition, thereby taking more of the market share. Within the architecture industry, AI and robotics are a part of this, and even quite basic software improvements have disrupted old systems. I can now click a couple of buttons to obtain my door schedule, saving me hours of work, but also taking away chargeable time from a technician. Another example is RESI, an 80-person firm focusing on residential architecture projects. It shows that to make good money from small-scale domestic work, you need to be a large firm with big efficiencies (such as meetings being online only, using technicians for a large portion of the work). How do you compete with that if you are aiming at the domestic market? By offering something different. Something more personal, bespoke, fun (such as Pride Road Architects in Chapter 10, Case Study 7). What could you disrupt?

THE MARKETING PYRAMID

Most architectural advertising is aimed at the people who already know they need an architect, but what if you could get on someone's radar and stay there before and when they finally do need an architect? This is the power of the marketing pyramid.

Basically, by aiming at the top Conversion section (see diagram above), as most do, there is far more competition, for fewer clients. If you develop a relationship (perhaps through networking, social media or blogging), then you can target the people in the bottom Awareness section (where most people sit) who don't even know they have a problem yet (e.g. lack of space can be solved by an architect, not just Ikea). The middle stage is the Information stage, for people who know they have a problem, are actively finding solutions, but have no idea who they should choose and perhaps even if they need an architect or just a builder. This is where information blogs and emails to your list are really powerful. You are informing them about different aspects of their project, perhaps through case studies, articles about planning issues, maybe a technical problem that you overcame. They will start to know and trust you, meaning you are unlikely to be compared to others when they are ready to appoint an architect.

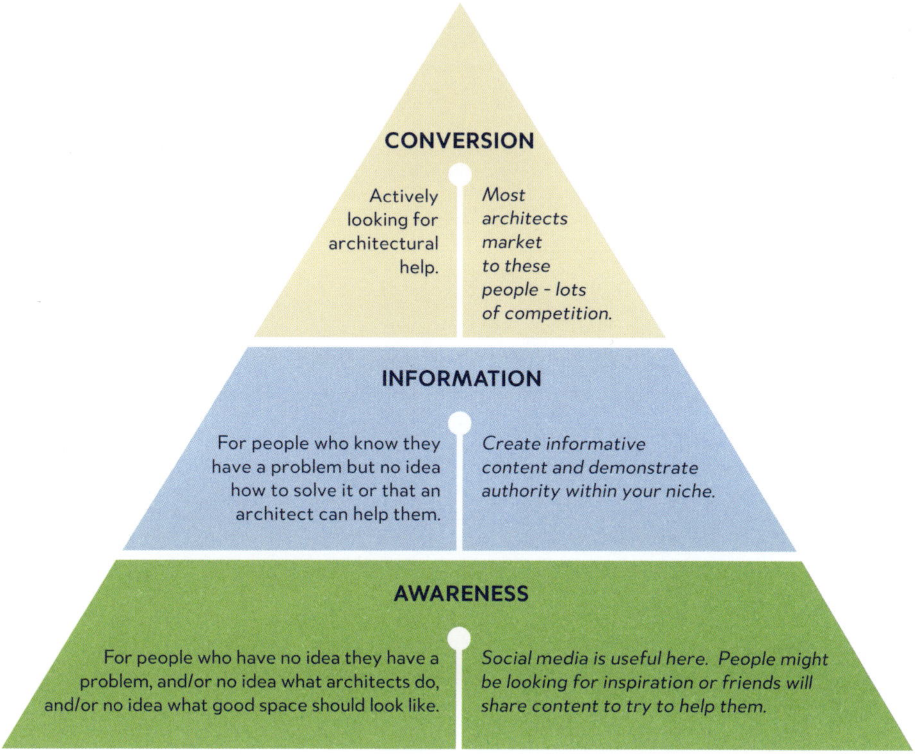

FIGURE 6.5 The Marketing Pyramid adapted for architects, showing Awareness, Information and Conversion sections

WINNING WORK

It is worth looking into multiple ways of winning work. The options listed below are all complementary, but you might find you are better at some than others.

Winning work via networking

I have found networking events to be a great way of meeting other business owners and sharing stories and advice. I have learnt a great deal and found people who can help me with different aspects of my business. I have also gained work – not as much as my website, but still worth having!

Winning work via referrals

We do receive referrals via happy clients or networking. Some of these are wonderful projects and others are not quite so well-suited to our values.

Winning work via your website

This is where 90% of our work comes from. I have explained my strategy for winning work via a website at the beginning of this chapter. If you think

FIGURE 6.6 An Instagram post demonstrating that eco-homes come in all forms

about how most people look for architects, it is via Google, but many gather inspiration using Pinterest and Instagram, and you can use these to raise your profile and attract more people to your website. This is especially useful when Google has not ranked you that high yet.

Social Media

We use different social media (SM) platforms for different things. Our blogs and website bring in plenty of work, so SM is really the icing on the cake or it is used with different aims.

We tend to use Instagram as a kind of background story. We add photos of us on site, at team meetings, designing collaboratively. We also add random images to represent what we like doing outside architecture.

The idea is to give a kind of CNA flavour, offering an idea of – or ethos and the atmosphere at – CNA, as well as how we work.

Twitter is mainly used to connect with other professionals. It is especially useful to get to know people before and after conferences and to ask for opinions or advice. We post blog and newsletter links on there. Nothing beats meeting people in real life to begin a relationship, but Twitter is useful for building on that and maintaining that relationship between events. If you work on public buildings, you might find Twitter is more useful for finding work. This could also apply if you offer a different service to those within the same industry.

It's easy to lose track of what you have posted, where and when. I keep a simple spreadsheet tracker. This also makes life easier when copying content on to different channels. People don't tend to remember what you posted last year, so it's also useful to be able to re-use content easily the following year.

Facebook is a funny one because we have very little traffic, but as one marketing person told me, it is familiar to everyone. If you don't have an easy to use website, Facebook is much easier for a client to get a flavour of what you do. New enquiries sometimes appear via this platform, so it's worth having. It's important to remove any barriers to a client making that first contact.

LinkedIn is another useful platform for posting blogs and connecting with other businesses (more so than domestic clients). However, during the absence of real networking in lockdown, I have found LinkedIn to be a useful boost on raising awareness of what we do. It's not much extra work, as we already have blogs we can use, but it reaches a wider audience who may not yet be searching for an architect, or even think they need one!

Email List

Building up your email list (and emailing them!) is a fantastic way to build up a steady flow of incoming, almost converted, leads. You might, as we do, offer a free eBook as an incentive to sign up to your list. Or it might just be an offer of a newsletter, keeping people up to date with the latest planning changes in your niche, for example.

If you are struggling for ideas for website/blog/email or SM content, look at magazines for inspiration. Depending on your niche, you might look at *Real Homes* magazine, *Country Life*, *The Economist*, *enki* or *Real Estate*. These magazines are trying to attract an audience, as are you. Take note of their cover headlines, as these will draw your clients in too.

BE A BIT FLEXIBLE AND DEFINITELY NOT PERFECT

In summary, it is best to just get going and start testing the market. The key takeaways are:

- Work out who your ideal client is and find out as much about them as possible.
- Be authentic.
- Demonstrate client benefits and outcomes, not a list of services.
- Don't make it easy to differentiate only on price.

CHAPTER 7

Easy mistakes and how to avoid them

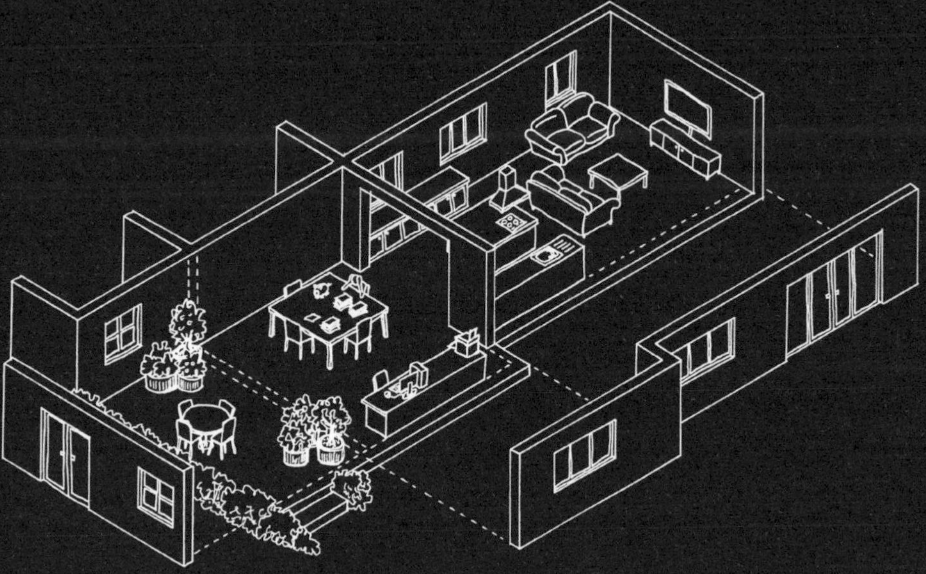

FIGURE 7.1 Mistakes happen but overall purpose will pull you through. This eco self-build project was huge fun to work on.

MISTAKE NO. 1: LOW FEES

In 2016, I was looking at yet another year on a low income, despite work coming out of my ears, and this no longer made sense. My fees were too low.

To put it into context, my earnings at that time were on par with data on sole practitioner salaries. Despite the huge compensations in lifestyle with working for yourself, at this time I would have earned more working full-time in a practice. That seemed daft. If I could be in control of my life, why not my income?

Hypnotherapy and business coaching helped me to understand how much financial benefit (notwithstanding the huge pleasure of living in their dream home) I was giving to my clients, but was I rewarding myself enough? When a client can make £200,000 in pure profit on a development project that I designed, it made my fees at that time look extremely silly. What was holding me back from charging reasonable fees? Through coaching I discovered:

- I had a big fear of disappointing clients and not being good enough, despite successful projects proving otherwise – imposter syndrome, too
- I feared losing work if I priced too highly: we don't have a set fee scale in the UK for architects
- I didn't understand how valuable I was to my client
- I feared that I would price out my 'nice' poorer clients and have to work only with 'scary' rich people (why do rich people have to be scary, incidentally?)
- my need to believe that 'architecture and good design should be available to everyone'.

I have personally really struggled with not being able to help everyone. I have always felt that good design should be for all. To keep a practice like mine going, the profit is only there on the higher-end projects. On small fees, you only need to over-run by a day and you have lost money. I have learnt that supporting myself first is not selfish. Far from it. If I thrive, I enable others to thrive as well. I can continue to employ really talented architects and watch them flourish. It means I can put energy into projects that make a difference to the world, as well as through books, teaching and research. Aiming at clients with a higher spend has also helped my eco-niche to grow. Those looking to stay in a home for 20 years are far more likely to spend more on eco-technologies. This helps us to learn more, put this into research and we will eventually discover more tools that can be applied to reduce energy and improve health in buildings more widely. Other innovative practices touch more people by having effective systems and high numbers of clients (see Chapter 10) or working on public projects where many benefit. I could have opted for either of those but chose this path because this is where my main interests lie and where I think I can make the biggest difference.

Money Blocks

There are so many of these, learnt in childhood or at architecture school, that prevent you charging what you are worth. I finally realised that I needed to commit to doubling my fees, otherwise I would be continually 'just scraping by', unable to save, putting myself and my family at financial risk. Not only this, I began to understand that wanting more money is not greedy. I am not materialistic and don't need 'things' or the status associated with a big car or the latest technology to make me happy. However, what I didn't understand was that money gives you choices. And choices mean freedom, a value that I rate extremely highly. Money gives you the ability to travel, to choose to work for a charity, to choose to save for rainy days, thus giving you security to work at your best, to be able to offer my husband a change of career, to choose to investigate other business ventures, to choose to spend time with (future) children. There were endless possibilities, all of them very exciting and none of them greedy.

You may find income does not increase straightaway: my practice, for instance, had existing projects on the old fee that we had to honour. However, around 10 months later I started to see a real difference, and no fewer clients got in contact. The quality of enquiries increased. I have since put up my fees again. I give fixed fees for all stages, no hourly rates (apart from unforeseen extra work), because as a rule clients don't care how many hours their architect works; they want a price for a result. Some services still have prices displayed on our website but I no longer show all fees, because I want clients to understand the value before seeing the price. Aiming at a higher end of the market means only very few enquiries expect to pay low fees. We can weed these out in the initial qualification. If I were to do it again, I would absolutely put all my fees on my website exactly as I used to. It helped me to win clients and saved me a lot of hassle with potential time-wasters. I am now aiming at a different target market because of my overall long-term goals.

It is an ongoing struggle. I have lost count of the times I have given myself some tough love, overridden my discounting mindset and just pressed 'send'. Then the client just comes back with 'yes, fine'. All that agonising – for nothing!

MISTAKE NO. 2: NOT HAVING A CASH-FLOW FORECAST

One of the things I would change about how I started my business would be to get the financial side sorted first. If only I had realised what a huge difference a simple cash-flow forecast spreadsheet would have had – not only on my own salary but also for understanding how many new jobs to take on and when. This reduces stress and, in my case, led to higher turnover. My cash-flow spreadsheet is linked to my outgoings, staff wages and profit plan. Every small change can be seen from all angles and understood. It's also a great 'what if' machine. What if I take on another employee? What if I raise her salary? What if I take on that project?

It is essential to include your own salary! I didn't do this for years and, funnily enough, I had to make do with the leftovers. These were mostly not as much as I hoped, but if you don't put in a goal to aim for, it just won't happen. So it didn't. For years. It is so important to pay yourself first. Businesses are not easy to run and it's important to feel rewarded. What's even more galling looking back is that I knew these rules of thumb, understood why they were important, and yet I still resisted. Financial analytics give you a lot of understanding, and that is very helpful for freeing up creativity. The important thing is to have a turnover goal each month that properly pays you as well as the business. The more you stick your head in the sand on the financials, the more likely it is that you will run out of cash.

I know I am good at marketing, creating a big vision, coming up with lots of ideas, business direction and solving problems creatively. Conversely, I know I am weak on data and detailed tasks, as well as project management and financial management. This is no surprise to me, as I would never have chosen these jobs for myself. As a small business owner, you have to wear all the 'hats' initially, until you can afford for someone else to help you. I have a tendency to just wing it in life: just getting on with things. I prefer trial and error. This is an excellent method for marketing or any kind of creative work. It simply does not work for financial or project management. I have tried and failed on this one. Planning and good data are key for healthy finances. There is no escape from that. Good strategies are charging clients a fixed percentage of the overall fee monthly. This saves hassle and invoice delays. We find charging 50% upfront helps considerably with project risk and cash-flow certainty.

I haven't been able to delegate all of these things yet, but I have super help from Jaina, an architect who loves this part. I also use apps and pre-set spreadsheets to help me get the analysis I need quickly and less painfully. There is more about this in Chapter 8.

MISTAKE NO. 3: STRESS AND BEING OVERWHELMED

One of the downsides of working for yourself is checking your own drawings. I find it draining to pick up detail. Working alone, it is very hard to look at a project with fresh eyes when you are wholly involved with it.

For two years I employed a freelance architect to check over drawings at building control stage. He was our second pair of eyes as well as having useful experience on similar projects. This, combined with our building regulations checklist, reduced our stress quite considerably. Now we have a bigger, more experienced team, including more detail-oriented architects, and we have the capacity to check each other's work.

Partly to keep costs down but also out of a sense of pride, I didn't reach out to other architects or consultants as soon as I should have. The weeks I have spent worrying about an architectural problem could have often been sorted in a day (and was!) if I had only spoken to a knowledgeable person sooner. We now use several consultants for various tasks, and for business expertise too. We have learnt from all of them and this ties in very well with our aim to always be at the forefront of the latest research and best practice.

Taking on too much work

I still remember that summer in 2014 when suddenly it all went boom. I received a commission for a book, I was offered a technology tutor role at Oxford Brookes and suddenly, in September, I found myself with 20 new clients (the increase in clients was explained by my new website and blogs, see Chapter 6). I was working all my evenings and weekends on top of normal working hours. From September to February, I only took Christmas day off. Unsurprisingly, I made myself quite ill. Something had to change.

Running a successful business takes a lot of time. Having started in the recession, I found it very hard to say no to work. At that time, I also did not have proper financial management or a cash-flow system in place. This made predicting workflow nigh on impossible. I only knew I wasn't earning enough money and I was working too many hours.

Eventually I put my health and good quality work before client pressures. It seems strange to me now. Why did I accept time constraints from clients who had no knowledge of the industry or the time it takes to create their dream home?

It is very important to:

- gain more confidence in yourself
- put good quality work before client pressures
- take regular time off.

Through coaching I learnt to always ask myself, 'Who is benefitting here?' It certainly wasn't me benefitting from working those long hours and, really, neither were my clients, as they certainly weren't getting my best creative input. I love my work, but to make intelligent decisions (often under pressure), I need time off. Every weekend. Every evening.

MISTAKE NO. 4: ASSUMING CLIENTS UNDERSTAND EVERYTHING

Planning reports are often written in confusing ways for a layperson; it's easy to forget how much is unclear to the client. Unless it is all positive, the reports need careful interpretation and explanation. This is very valuable to the client and something they may not know they need before going through the process.

In the early days, I did not recognise how much more I understood about planning reports than the client. Therefore, I was confused when a client replied that he was disappointed with the outcome of a pre-application. It was a positive result! There were some 'no's, but also plenty of 'yes's, and I could visualise what could be done within the 'yes's. Of course, that is part of our unique ability as architects, to design within constraints. However, it's important to make sure the client understands this and that planning reports are summarised and interpreted for them.

We like to test out ideas with the planners before launching into an expensive design process with a client. I will now explain in some detail the potential or expected outcomes of the planning process. There is lots of information about what a pre-application is and what it means on my website. We include the same information in our welcome pack. I also learnt about how much clients viewed me as their support mechanism through tricky planning regulations and a building project. Since then, we have always worked hard to be as transparent as possible about our approach and the potential pitfalls along the way.

Other things that worry clients are timescales and when you need paying! This is all set out clearly in our appointment emails and terms. I have found it simpler to split project stages up into smaller steps. It's easier for clients to understand what has changed and it means more regular cash flow for us. Each stage has bullet points of what they can expect. We also have a timescale chart, showing the average time taken for different types of projects. Clients don't expect us to always stick to that, but it gives them a good guide and reduces the number of repeat questions we receive.

MISTAKE NO. 5: GIVING AWAY TOO MUCH ADVICE FOR FREE

It is really important that clients know they are in the right place from the outset. This saves time as well as giving clients all the information they need to make a decision to contact you. Architects have all kinds of different ways of reducing wasted time on winning work. Harrison Stringfellow Architects (see Chapter 10, Case Study 2) use a questionnaire and an information pack to reduce pointless visits. Others don't charge for a first visit, knowing that if the job is interesting enough, it's worth the time just getting in front of the client. It's important to use your judgement here and to know your market. I have wasted much time on sketches for jobs that were only for low fees anyway. A friend of mine often sketches with potential clients and leaves the drawings with the client. On a few occasions, the client has used a cheaper technician to bring her ideas into fruition. That is very frustrating! If that is the kind of market you are in, you could accept that and create your systems and business model around it as the Pride Road Architects has done (see Chapter 10, Case Study 7).

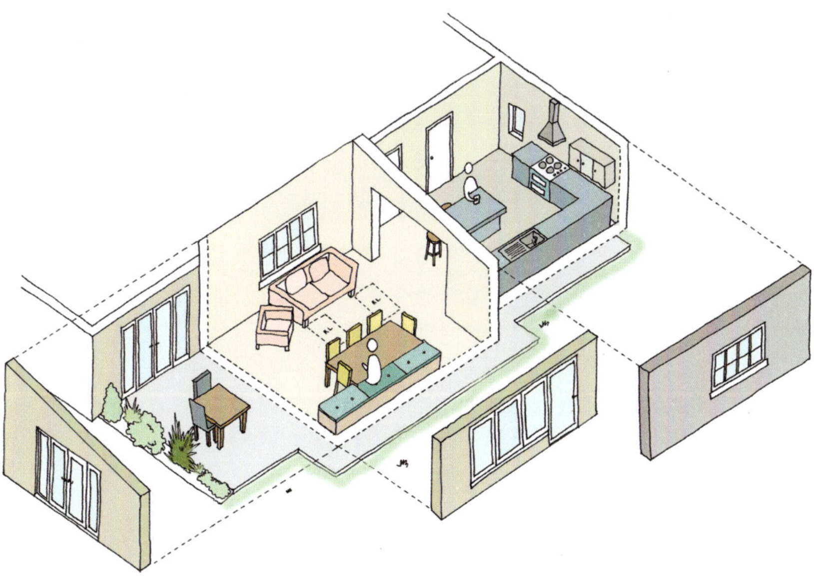

FIGURE 7.2 Example of a sketch service drawing

Or you could move into a more lucrative market. We now charge for initial consultations, as we provide a lot of value to the client in those. Sometimes people base quite big life decisions on our advice! We take the cost off the project if they go ahead with us. At peak times I can spend a lot of time on these visits, preparing for each one, following up with advice and costs, so it's important to feel rewarded and valued for this work.

MISTAKE NO. 6: HOW I RESCUED MY BUSINESS FROM NEARLY GOING UNDER

This is something that continues to hang over me, even though I have come to understand that this wasn't a business failure. In 2017 we still had an offer that people wanted to buy. It was simply that the website wasn't performing as it should, so we had far fewer leads coming in. I didn't realise that the August lull that we always have would not bounce back in September/October as it always does, because the website was not functioning properly.

This was compounded by the timing. I was in the latter stages of pregnancy and trying to train up my team as much as I could. I knew I would need to reduce my hours once the baby arrived. Once baby did arrive, I didn't have the energy to spot IT problems or to sort them. I was focused on looking after existing clients and making sure the architectural process didn't suffer as a consequence of my shorter hours. I felt that was the biggest potential disaster – an architectural problem could have caused client distress and lost us a lot of money. I falsely relied on my website to do well, as it always had done. I find marketing and website tech easy, so this seemed something that I could rely on.

These are all the things that happened in sequence, compounding to make CNA finances plummet and two months of reduced hours for staff. My earnings dropped enormously too.

1. My website theme was no longer being kept up to date by the developer, which caused a number of issues; one of which was a very slow to load website. This put off many potential leads.
2. The SSL certificate had stopped working – Google did not favour my website in Google rankings.
3. At sales meetings, clients were put off by my pregnancy. They didn't fully understand that I have a team, nor that parenting would be shared between my husband and me. Consequently, I didn't win as much work as usual prior to my baby's arrival.
4. Two large jobs were delayed and then halted due to lack of funds.
5. I simply had no time for marketing on top of architecture in the first few weeks after my baby was born.

6. The Beast from the East in early 2018 seriously affected potential clients' inclination to start a project. It affected estate agents as well, who didn't see house sales spike until May, two months later than usual.
7. In January, we usually receive around 15 to 20 enquiries. In January 2018, we had only three enquiries, in February only four, and so on.

Recovery

I felt incredibly guilty – I should have been able to foresee all of this and protect my staff. However, I had great transparency with my team and the good relationship we had cultivated really saw us through this period. Staff reduced their hours for two months – in fact, this worked out fortuitously, as two employees were completing their studies and needed extra time off and one employee had just taken on an extra research post and was wondering how she could fit it all in. Other than reducing salary outgoings, these are the major steps I took to orchestrate a recovery:

1. My husband supported me to work weekends and evenings to win more work and complete more work to get cash into the business
2. The 3Fs Business Mentoring Programme, run by Chris Gardener, really helped me to understand what my clients really wanted. It enabled me to set up new services and attract new clients quickly. While re-building my website I networked more, to speed up getting the word out.
3. I could not afford to invest in a better website but the theme needed changing, and I knew that done badly, this could be disastrous to existing content, so I paid an expert for this small chunk (£250).
4. I got professional photos of the team organised. Clients felt reassured by our smiling faces and this brought in more work.
5. In small but frequent chunks I updated the website. Starting again helped me to focus even more on what the client wants to read, who I was aiming at and what I wanted to make most prominent.
6. In September 2018 we had 18 new enquiries and it has been consistent since then.

In tough times, it's important to go through the financials and cut out any unnecessary expenses. It's important to understand the causes and evaluate if they are short- or long-term problems. Then you can plan your strategy to overcome them:

- If you have a team, don't hide the problems, they may have good ideas to help.
- Although tempting, it's not always best to throw money at the problem (such as a brand new website which would have cost me £6,000); there can be creative solutions that have a big impact for small cost.
- Apply Pareto's 80/20 rule here (see Chapter 8).

FIGURE 7.3 Sketch service drawing of a bungalow modernisation

- Don't stick your head in the sand, look at it all in gritty detail and seek help with the parts that are outside of your expertise.
- Look for the things that are in your control (for me this was sorting the website problems) and those outside of your control which may just need patience to overcome (such as my baby bump having a negative effect on sales, or Covid-19).

IF I WERE TO START AGAIN, WHAT WOULD I DO DIFFERENTLY?

Due to redundancy, I set up in practice with no clients. Ideally, I would have set up, perhaps with a partner, with a clear idea of what I wanted to do, rather than just something to pay the bills. It took me longer than it needed to earn good money because of that. On the other hand, it can be very hard to make that leap into sole practice without a big push. Redundancy, followed by freelancer isolation, were my big pushes.

I would also have a financial plan from the outset. I should have got input from an accountant on how to set up a good cash-flow forecast.

Starting up with a partner could have helped me to reduce some of the pressure that was, and still is, solely on me a lot of the time (though the benefits are enormous freedom). Starting again, I would either do this or I would network right from the beginning to find my support team, such as business coaches, specialists in marketing, finance and project management, as well as building industry consultants and eco-specialists.

I am now in my tenth year of my own practice. It shows that mistakes happen, but you can overcome them and thrive.

CHAPTER 8

Systems and efficiencies

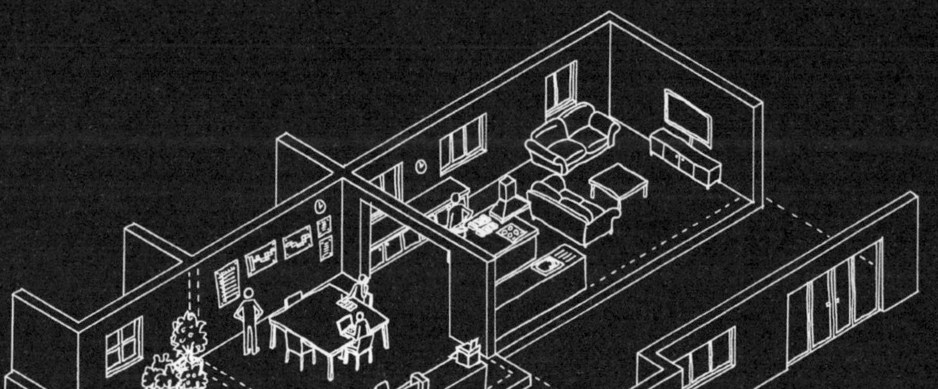

FIGURE 8.1 An example of a project worked on using 3D Vectorworks

Early into running my practice, I read the *E-Myth Revisited: Why most small businesses don't work and what to do about it* by Michael Gerber. The central idea – that systems enable a more profitable business, less hamster wheel busy-ness and more time for your best work – made a lot of sense to me. I started creating systems for myself and for others when I started employing. Now we do this as a team, which eases the burden and ensures we develop systems that work for all.

As a creative I had avoided checklists (despite making quite detailed to-do lists each day!). After hearing Mark R. LePage on the EntreArchitect podcast explain how better efficiency equals more time for creativity, I finally overcame my rebellious mindset and developed some useful checklists of my own.

Creating systems is a handy discipline which will also benefit the sole trader and enable some of it to be outsourced to a virtual assistant or similar. I would highly recommend a VA, even if you don't want to employ staff. They will make a much better job of certain tasks than you, have good suggestions for improving processes and crucially free up your time to do the things that actually allow you to make money – good architecture and business direction. Some examples of things that virtual assistants can do for architects:

- be a first point of contact for clients
- manage all client data and enquiry lists
- prepare appointment documents
- email clients with pre-set text for recurring enquiries
- organise files
- set up new files
- prepare spreadsheets for your analysis
- research new software or systems and prepare a pros and cons list
- upload receipts to accounting software

- invoice management
- liaise payroll details with the accountant
- help with onboarding of a new employee with contracts and wayfinding
- organise your diary and book in client appointments (and work out travel times) for you.

SALES SYSTEMS

Sales Pipeline

There are all kinds of sales pipeline software available. Some are aimed at large businesses with a hefty price tag to cover the super-whizzy extras they offer. One of the downsides of remote working is that you cannot share a machine for expensive software that staff don't need access to regularly (e.g. Photoshop). It can get pricey if you need multiple users. So instead of a bells-and-whistles sales pipeline software, my office uses Trello, a project management tool used to create boards, and cards and notes within these boards. We have a 'PotJobs' (potential jobs) board where we log incoming enquiries. Within this board are a series of cards with titles like: New Enquiry, Enquiry Form Sent, Meeting Booked, Pricing Sent, Pricing Follow up, Went Elsewhere, Project Abandoned, Not Suitable. If they become a live project, then they get their own client board and the card with their information and correspondence is copied over to the new board. Rebecca, our VA, manages this board and pastes over any email correspondence and phone call outcomes. It's really efficient and allows us to keep tabs on who to follow-up. Quite often a client will make an enquiry and not go ahead for some time. This enables us to catch up quickly when they do go ahead with us. Capsule and HubSpot are others that small businesses use for sales pipeline and CRM management.

I began using a virtual receptionist in 2019. I have no idea what took me so long to appoint one. It's incredibly simple, highly efficient and extremely cheap. Previously my home phone operated as the business landline. I hate being interrupted by phone calls and it is a bad idea for me to answer the phone because as soon as the enquirer realises they have got 'Clare', if I am not careful I disappear down a rabbit hole of architectural queries with no project at the end of it. For a long time, I simply let the answer machine go off and asked Rebecca to call them back as per our sales process above. However, the noise of the phone ringing was very distracting and I couldn't help but overhear messages. Today, a professional person answers the phone, takes a message and sends us an email. It also provides a much more professional image. Not everyone likes answerphones, and some people prefer to call than email. This process catches all of those.

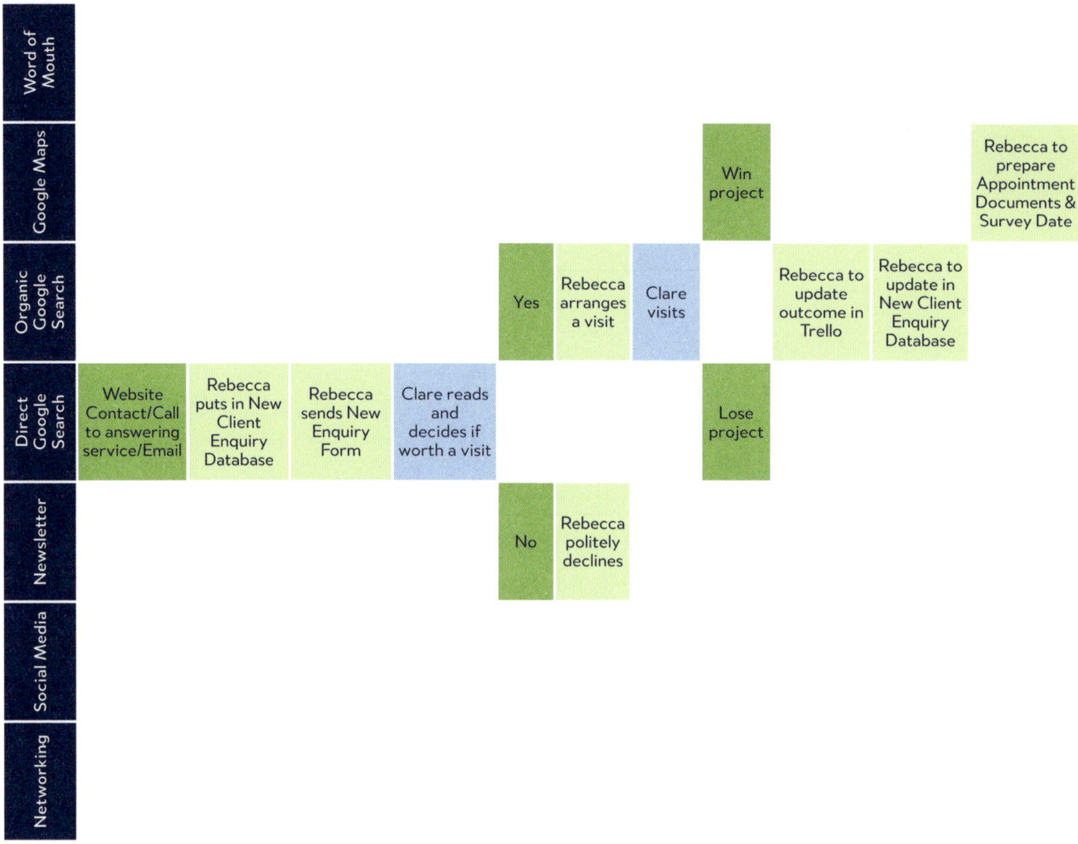

FIGURE 8.2 Our sales process

Pre-Qualification process

Like Harrison Stringfellow Architects, a practice in Liverpool (see Chapter 10, Case Study 2), we use a pre-qualification questionnaire. This reduces enormously the wasted sales visits. It also enables me to find out more about the potential client before visiting, so that I can prepare more easily for their questions. The questionnaire itself is used to establish their priorities and budget. It also has a key question about their attitude to sustainability – important to our specialism. We don't want to just preach to the converted, but a willingness to be open to ideas is important in a future client.

CLIENT SYSTEMS

I would thoroughly recommend working with a virtual assistant to relieve a lot of the admin associated with client appointments and queries. Rebecca takes away all the hassle of initial enquiries, diary management, appointment documents and keeps spreadsheets up to date. After the virtual receptionist (VR), she is the first person that clients speak to. It reduces the volume of emails that I get and takes a whole set of thinking away from me.

We find it is helpful to have a welcome pack to send out to clients. It explains the whole process of working with us, including timescales and our unusual office set-up. It also covers many of our frequently asked questions, reducing time later.

TEAM/PROJECT MANAGEMENT SYSTEMS

Initially, all team communication was done by email. Now the office uses Slack, an app for team communication. It is like an instant messaging app but with threads sorted into channels. For us these are project channels as well as office management, marketing and 'random' channels where we post interesting or funny items not directly relevant to the working channels. Straightaway this had the advantage of unclogging my inbox with staff queries. The whole team can now answer queries that are rarely just for me. Working flexibly means not all of us are available all of the time. By using a system like Slack, queries and information are available to the whole team wherever and whenever they are working. It's easy to set your working hours so that you are not disturbed outside these times. It's rare that anything is so super urgent that we need to bypass this. For that we use WhatsApp (about once every year!).

The whole team puts their availability in a Google calendar so that we can all see who is available when and meetings can be organised for us. The Google calendar also contains reminders for when to check in with planners and building control officers.

Every practice with a team will have a resourcing spreadsheet or system. Ours is called an 'invoicing schedule'. It morphed from the lists I would make in my notebook about when projects needed to be invoiced compared with time. We invoice at two-week intervals (for different clients) to ensure cash flow keeps flowing. It also helps to prioritise project work. The advantage of the Google spreadsheet is that everyone can see it, rather than it being stuck in my brain or notebook! Jaina now prepares this every month based on the projects' spreadsheet and the invoices list in Xero. It helps us all to see clearly how workload is looking and means that you don't overlook time spent on meetings, marketing and CPD as available project work time. There are project management apps that do some of this work for you. For now, this simple spreadsheet suits us.

FINANCIAL SYSTEMS

Sensible money practice

Sometimes rules are there to be broken; sometimes rules are a really good idea. Here are some really good ones regarding financial practice. Running your own business does not have to include all that stress if you follow these rules.

- Pay yourself first – this is a healthy mindset, because it puts your needs first and makes sure you receive reward for your business efforts. If you feel rewarded, you feel happier and you attract more clients.
- Put aside your tax and VAT after paying yourself – then you know what is left for expenses and salaries. This makes you hustle for the rest of the money each month. Paying the above last means you always end up with leftovers and panic when VAT and tax payments are due.
- Charge 50% upfront for all services (thereby splitting your risk with the client 50%, as well as ensuring good cash flow and payment delays caused by others, such as client delay, waiting on consultants or planners).
- Consider charging a set monthly fee to clients that comes out automatically (GoCardless can do this for you).
- Ensure you maintain what I call a good 'Basic Numbers' spreadsheet (see below) so you understand what your turnover needs to be and can adjust quickly when things change, such as taking on a new member of staff or an additional expense.
- Keep a good cash-flow forecast.
- Scan in receipts frequently using a scanning app like Scannable that scans directly using your phone to Evernote. Ask a VA to upload them to your financial software system; this means you have up-to-date financial status at any time. Other scanner apps exist for other note apps like One Note.

Life and Death by cash-flow forecast

I started with a cash-flow spreadsheet and there are many examples online. However, as an architect I find it very useful to include a project management tool within it. The spreadsheet doesn't simply show money coming in and out of the business, it also shows project stage and fee for each stage. Today, the office has maintained the projects spreadsheet as a quick tool to play around with workload vs fee income per month. Over time, I found it tiresome to input manually. The cash-flow forecast is now in a separate app called Float, which directly links to our Xero accounting software. This data existed in Xero already (I moved to online accounting after three years in business when I was managing too many clients), so it made sense to export it into a cash-flow app. There are also project management apps out there that combine all of this together but, for the moment, this is a very cost-effective and time-efficient way for us to manage a small business. If we grow, I will probably invest in something like Harvest, a project management and time-tracking app, with many useful plug-ins offering cash-flow forecasting and more.

Figure 8.3 is an example of the spreadsheet cash-flow forecast.

It has all of our clients on the left-hand side, then all the months in a financial year across the top. In each month I insert the expected invoice amount for each client, colour-coded according to the project stage. Once we have won a project, all the fee information is loaded on to the cash-flow forecast. Below the client list are rows that relate to items in the Basic Numbers spreadsheet. Outgoings are listed on a separate sheet to be updated when necessary. The totals are then linked to the cash-flow spreadsheet.

At a glance, you can see how full your workload is for that month. I can see in advance when we have too much or too little work to meet our turnover target. I can also move project fee stages around according to our workload or client pressures. I can see when it would be good to employ another team member, or when we will finally have some spare time to write blogs. I can see if we need to do more marketing in order to get further work in for three months' time. It's incredibly useful: it's the one spreadsheet that tells you an enormous amount about the health of your business, right now and in the future.

Clearly, good marketing, quality of the team and our architectural skills make the business a success, but without this cash-flow system everything would fall to pieces. It is the number one thing I would put in place if starting a business again from scratch.

PROJECT	April	May	June	July	August	September	October	November	December	January	February	March	TOTALS
Business Opening Balance	£3.000	£1.150	£4.470	£2.660	£4.460	£7.610							
Job #1			£700			£2.500							£3.200
Job #1				£1.500									£1.500
Job #2	£3.000				£2.500	£2.500							£8.000
Job #3	£1.500					£2.000							£3.500
Job #4		£1.150											£1.150
Job #5	£1.900												£1.900
Job #6	£1.500												£0
Job #7		£1.000	£1.500										£1.500
Job #8			£2.000	£2.250									£4.250
Job #9	£2.000			£1.200	£2.500								£5.700
Job #10			£2.000	£2.000	£2.000	£2.000							£8.000
Job #11	£500												£0
Job #12		£600	£2.500		£2.000								£4.500
Job #13	£1.500	£2.500			£2.000	£2.000							£8.000
Job #14			£1.000	£1.000									£2.000
Job #15		£1.200											£1.200
Job #16	£1.000	£1.000											£1.000
Job #17			£1.800	£500	£800	£950							£4.050
Job #18		£1.000	£2.000			£2.500							£5.500
Sketch service													
Other income streams			£120	£40	£300	£450							
Monthly revenue	£12.900	£8.450	£13.620	£8.490	£12.100	£14.900	£0	£0	£0	£0	£0	£0	£61.970
VAT	£2.580	£1.690	£2.724	£1.698	£2.420	£2.980	£0	£0	£0	£0	£0	£0	
Employee salaries+hmrc	£5.000	£5.000	£5.000	£5.000	£5.000	£5.000	£5.000	£5.000	£5.000	£5.000	£5.000	£5.000	£55.000
Payroll + pensions	£11.00	£1.100	£1.100	£1.100	£1.100	£1.100	£1.100	£1.100	£1.800	£1.800	£1.800	£1.800	
My salary (net)	£3.000	£3.000	£3.000	£3.000	£3.000	£3.000	£3.000	£3.000	£3.000	£3.000	£3.000	£3.000	£36.000
Outgoings	£2.300	£2.300	£2.300	£2.300	£2.300	£2.300	£2.300	£2.300	£2.300	£2.300	£2.300	£2.300	£27.600
Big bills						£1.450							

FIGURE 8.3 An example of a cash-flow and projects forecast

	September	October	November	December	January	February	March	April
Job #1	£2.500		£7.500					
Job #2	£3.000	£2.500	£2.000	£2.000				
Job #3		£1.500		ENGINEER	BUILD C			
Job #4		£0						
Job #5	£500							
Job #6	£900	£900						
Job #7	£300	£800	£900	£6000			ENGINEER	BUILD C
Job #8	£1.350		DETAILS					
Job #9	£2.500	£900	£2.000	£1.200	£2.000			
Job #10			ENGINEER	BUILD C				
Job #11								
Job #12		£1.000						
Job #13	£1.500		£1.500					
Job #14		£200	£300					
Job #15	£600							
Job #16	£500		£900					
Job #17	£700							
Job #18		£800	£950	£750	£750			
Job #19	£0	£2.500	£2.000					
Job #20		£600	£3.500	£2.000				
Job #21	£250	£3.500	£6.500	£4.500	£350			
Total	£14.600	£15.200	£28.050	£16.450	£3.100	£0	£0	£0
VAT	£2.920	£3.040	£5.610	£3.290	£620	£0	£0	£0
Total inc VAT	£17.520	£18.240	£33.660	£19.740	£3.720	£0	£0	£0

PRE-APP	SURVEY	ONE DESIGN	PLANNING	RESEARCH	ENGINEER
BUILD C	ECO SERVICES	SS	DETAILS	SITE VISIT	

FIGURE 8.4 A simple project forecast

There is a saying, 'Turnover is Vanity, Profit is Sanity, Cash is Reality'. 'Cash is King' is another one. The sayings allude to the fact that you can have a high turnover but you might be making zero profit. That is unhealthy for business, especially if you are a sole trader and the profit is your income. You can also have a healthy profit, but if it all comes in three months after your bills are due, it's not much help. That's why cash is king. It keeps things flowing through the business. Businesses can go under very quickly without good cash flow.

Finally, I create a Basic Numbers spreadsheet with the following headings:

- Salaries
- Freelancers
- Payroll costs
- Pension costs
- My salary
- Tax savings
- Profit
- Total and Total plus VAT.

It's really important to separate your own salary, I find. It makes it more prominent and therefore non-forgettable!

BASICS	Monthly	Yearly
Salaries (net)	£2.800	£33.600
Payroll	£500	£6.000
V.A	£300	£3.600
Pensions	£150	£1.800
Director Salary (net)	£3.000	£36.000
Tax savings	£1.000	£12.000
Expenses	£2.000	£24.000
Total	£9.750	£117.000
Profit	£975	£11.700
New Total	£10.725	£128.700
VAT	£2.145	£25.740
New Total	£12.870	£154.440
Break Even (£2000 Director Salary and no profit)	£8.750	
inc VAT	£10.500,0	

FIGURE 8.5 A Basic Numbers spreadsheet using example figures for a small firm. Salaries figure include one architect and one part-time architectural assistant.

At a glance it tells me the turnover that I need to aim for each month. Below this, I also have a break even rate. This tells me how much I need to get in to pay the bills. It helps me not to worry if we are a bit delayed on invoicing some work, if I know it will come in only a week later than planned. The important thing is to have a turnover goal each month that properly pays you as well as the business. If you don't have a destination, you can't steer the ship!

This turnover number also enables me to work backwards to find out my practice daily charge-out rate. This simple calculation has enabled me to understand my pricing much better and to stop discounting!

Again, you work backwards. Put in the total working days available each month for each staff member, then take out average illness and holiday days. I also exclude marketing and business management time, as well as our office meetings. I then add up the total practice days available for architectural work, dividing the turnover required by the number of days. This gives me my daily practice charge-out rate. I then add on about 10% for unforeseen costs. It's worth testing this for a few months to check it's working out as you expected. You might need to adjust time spent on business (I frequently find I spend more than 50% of my time on business activities as a director) or add more than 10% for project over-run, especially when you are working on project types that are new to you.

Finance for taking on an employee or freelancer

My general approach was to reduce the initial financial load of an employee. All my employees started working one day a week at first. This is quite easy to save up for, in any healthy business. Then, after three months, I increased that to two or three days a week. When the first employee left, I replaced her with two part-time employees, managing five days between them. Other practices, such as Invisible Studio (see Chapter 10, Case Study 3), only use freelancers. Once a project fee is known, they can outsource a portion to freelancers.

VAT, tax and paying yourself first

You won't come across this when you first set up, but once your turnover

	Days Available/ month	Business/marketing time - 20% of architect time, 50% of director time	Holidays	Childcare	Illness	Office Meetings (half a day each)	Total days for architectural work/ Month	Turnover per month (ex VAT)	(turnover /days available for architectural work) ex VAT
Director x 1	20	10	2.3333	2	0.25	2	3.4167	£10,725	
Architect x 1	20	4	2.3333		0.5	2	11.1667		£531.8159
Assistant part-time	10	2	1.16665		0.25	1	5.58335		
Total Days							20.16675		

FIGURE 8.6 Daily charge-out rate

gets past a certain amount (£85,000 in 2020), you have to charge your customers VAT. You save this up and then pay back most of it to HMRC. Assuming you pay VAT on purchases for your business, you won't need to pay back all of the VAT. As a business that doesn't need to buy in stock (like most architects), we don't make many VAT savings. My accountant works all of this out for me. I wouldn't suggest trying it yourself. If you have hit a VAT-worthy turnover, you can afford an accountant anyway.

This can be tricky initially to get your head around – it certainly was for me. All of a sudden what was in my business account at the end of the month wasn't mine. It was HMRC's. It was tempting to spend it to ease cash flow (and it was helpful for this when I was rescuing the business). However, that is bad practice and will create lots of stress and drama further down the road. If you are a natural saver, you would possibly go the other way. A friend of mine was so afraid of not saving enough for VAT and tax payments that she kept herself quite poor for a year before realising it was not as bad as she thought. I now save away all of the VAT each month, before I even really know it is there. This stops me looking at my account with a false sense of security. That money isn't mine; I am just storing it for a while. That way, there is usually a bit leftover, which I treat as a business reserve. It's there for unexpected bills and rainy days. It makes me feel safer.

Being British, I have always struggled to talk about money, and this followed through to my invoicing practice. I often felt guilty about sending an invoice, which is utterly absurd when the work was complete and the client had already agreed to a fee schedule. I am now quite militant about payment. The 50% upfront came about because I finally realised the risk the business was taking by not doing this. The client, on the other hand, is working with a reputable, long-standing firm, yet I have only just met them! Sharing the risk with a 50% upfront invoice suddenly made sense.

ARCHITECTURAL SYSTEMS

CAD efficiencies

One of my biggest frustrations working on architectural projects was the lack of efficiency in the CAD systems used. I learnt Vectorworks while working as a freelancer, having previously used AutoCAD and MicroStation for some years. I found Vectorworks to be far more intuitive and more useful for designers, but working in 2D still frustrated me. All the lining up of the elevations/sections; every time there was a change, remembering to update every single drawing. Finally, I went on a one-day course in Vectorworks 3D. After this I drew up a survey of a house in 3D. Straightaway I saved a third of the time it would have taken me to draw up a similar size house in 2D! Today, with more practise and greater knowledge, I think it takes us approximately half the time it used to at all design stages. Plus, the best thing is that every time a client changes their mind, it is so quick and easy. It takes away a lot of that pain and frustration. This same ease of design changes enable options to be quickly explored, shown, accepted or rejected.

Younger readers will read the above and think, 'Why would you not use 3D automatically?' Whatever the technology, the important takeaway is not to get bogged down with thinking, 'This is how it has always been done.' Keep innovating and you will never get left behind. Technology is always changing the game, but there will always be a place for hand-drawing and making. It makes architecture human, because it is uniquely created by different people, rather than a machine. Clients are people, too, and will always feel drawn to this form of expression. The important thing is to keep questioning: is this the right system for me and my practice? Pay attention to the rest of the industry but apply it through your own personal filter. For example, AutoCAD is the industry standard, taught at most architecture schools. I personally find it very clunky and unpredictable. For the same price we use Vectorworks, which includes BIM and 3D (no exporting to Revit or SketchUp, which saves time). However, this system might not be appropriate for large projects. Use your own filter.

Drawing/Architecture systems

My practice begins all projects with a design questionnaire, filled out by the client. This enables us to establish all their likes and dislikes as well as their priorities. We combine this with Pinterest boards. Client briefs have pre-set questions so that nothing gets missed. We have a checklist to ensure we remember everything during all stages: survey, planning, building regulations. The latter contains a process on how to set up a drawing so that a new person could follow it. Then a more highly trained person can edit and check it. The checklist also ensures important parts are not missed. Whenever we get caught out, new things are added to the list, so it becomes more comprehensive with time.

TIME-MANAGEMENT SYSTEMS

Since applying the principles listed below, I normally only need to work a five-hour day. I am not just efficient in those short hours, but more effective. The difference is critical to understand. Some of the systems I use overlap, and some have different names in different books, but they amount to the same thing. I'm not perfect. Small and medium disasters regularly de-rail me, and too often I self-sabotage when things are going well. I get distracted by shiny exciting things that are not part of my mission. Then I breathe and pull myself back on track and back to this system.

Time/Strengths Systems – Making the most of your abilities and available time

Stephen Covey – 'start with the end in mind'

Stephen Covey's *The 7 Habits of Highly Effective People* is one of my favourite business books. In it, we are told that we should 'start with the end in mind'. There is not much point in a time-management system if you don't understand what you are trying to achieve. Having an overall goal helps you to prioritise and focus on what's important rather than what feels urgent (hello email). If you are a student, that goal might be to complete a module. For a project architect it could be completing a project on time. For a business owner it could be winning certain project types.

Mission

I have a mission to innovate tools to reduce energy use in buildings, for example. When something new lands on my to-do list – a new project, an opportunity, a book to read, a podcast – I can filter it through my mission statement. If it's not part of my mission statement and not part of giving me joy in my leisure time, it is removed from my to-do list. It's quite Marie Kondo actually!

80/20 rule

After this, I think about the 80/20 rule or the Pareto Principle. There's lots about this in Tim Ferriss books and blogs, but it basically means that there are many things you spend 80% of your time doing that only achieve 20% profit or 20% joy – ditch those! Conversely, if you can find the things that only take 20% of your time but have 80% effect in profit or fun, keep those.

Know your strengths

My strengths are in vision, innovation and marketing. When I was forced to work fewer hours due to having a newborn, these were the things I kept. Because they are how I make the biggest difference to my practice goals in the shortest amount of time. If you enjoy and are good at something, you are naturally faster. For example, I can write a blog in an hour – and some of these blogs are still bringing in top work six years later. That work turned out to be really effective! I spend a few hours at the beginning of every project sketching out ideas and potential problem scenarios, which ensures a much smoother ride for the rest of the team. I regularly attend technical conferences on eco-subjects which I then filter through into what we can use as a practice. It enables me to innovate and stay ahead. This is effective use of time.

Stephen Covey's scheduling 'roles'

When looking at my to-do list at the beginning of each week, I write lists under separate 'roles' à la Covey, e.g. Wife, Mother, Architect, Director, Marketing, Writer, Individual. This ensures family life and my own sanity are given equal priority with work tasks.

Focus on important work as well as the urgent

Covey also shows the Eisenhower Matrix in his book. There are many variables on titles for the individual 'quadrants' but essentially it helps you to prioritise the important over the urgent. I often fall back on it when feeling overwhelmed.

Schedule-in personal tasks first

Following Kate Northrup's advice in *Do Less: A Revolutionary Approach to Time and Energy Management for Busy Moms*, it is best to schedule in personal tasks first. I have to regularly remind myself of this, but it works really well when I do so. I put in exercise and cooking slots for each day (5pm family dinner-making duties come around super-fast when you are engrossed in work; planning is the only stress-free option here). Then I put in my diary appointments and then my business or architectural work time. I always keep Wednesdays meeting-free for breathing space.

Deep work and Shallow work

I highly recommend all of Cal Newport's books. *Deep Work: Rules for Focused Success in a Distracted World* is useful for understanding how you can be very efficient at work or at university. By grouping your work into 'deep work' (focused work) and 'shallow work' (admin/emails/meetings), it is much easier to organise your life and get more out of it. It gives you greater free time and less stress. I did this instinctively to allow me to fit in triathlon training around my studies, but I became very distracted again later on.

Newport's book brought me back on track.

Night Owl or Early Lark or in between?

Work out if you are an owl or a lark or in between – define your most productive time and schedule appropriately. For what I do, see Chapter 9.

Batch cook your to-do list

Another one from Tim Ferriss – grouping similar activities makes them faster. I apply this to making phone calls, batch cooking, batch email, uploading sketches, receipts and survey data. This saves me hours each week.

Check email only twice a day

Checking email or social media is 'shallow work' (see above) and therefore needs to be consciously slotted into smaller amounts of time. I find that I use email or social media to avoid difficult or uncomfortable tasks. It is good practice to check email only two to three times a day. I check it too often when I am anxious. The awareness of this has been useful. When I realise why I am doing it, I sort of go 'aha' and tackle the tricky task or try to address the root of the anxiety.

Creative types reading this may now be thinking, 'Gosh, what a lot of boring planning/scheduling!' I would have resisted this also, apart from the knowledge that drifting about 'being spontaneous' led to stress and non-achievement of goals. Over time, these tools become easy flow and with more time for the things I love, it makes me happier too. It now only takes me about 20 minutes at the start of each week. A far more effective week follows.

Ladies – make the most of your menstrual cycle

As mentioned, Kate Northrup has written a useful book called *Do Less*. This highlights how it benefits all of us (not just women) to work in a cyclical way, rather than from a daily or weekly to-do list. Due to hormones naturally present during different times of a woman's cycle, women will instinctively find they are far better at certain activities at different times of the month. Understanding this has felt like learning a new superpower. It has made a big difference to my productivity. For example, I book-in networking and talks when I will naturally feel more sociable. I book-in detailed tasks and finishing projects when I will be in the right mood (this is also a useful time for decluttering). I reduce meetings when I will need to rest more.

If this interests you, I recommend reading more about it in Northrup's book and on her website.

Resources

For daily scheduling I use bullet journaling on real paper, which I find very satisfying. https://bulletjournal.com/pages/learn

CHAPTER 9

Business and a baby

I knew that I wasn't full-time mum material from quite an early age. I have always been ambitious, and I knew I would struggle to give up that part of myself, but I really wanted to be a mum and to enjoy being one if I possibly could. Although I never expected a family to be guaranteed, I knew that with or without one I wanted a fulfilling career to fit around my life and not the other way around. I needed to be able to create this.

When I was planning how to run a business and keep a baby alive, I knew it would be hard. The reality was harder than I expected in some respects and much easier in others.

In late pregnancy and the early months of my son's life, I scoured the internet to find information about how other parents ran professional services businesses with a newborn. There were many tales of 'mumpreneurs' (mums who had created businesses while at home looking after small children). They all made it sound much easier than the reality must have been. There was practically nothing about keeping an established business going. I read about a lawyer going back to work when her baby was three weeks old – but she had a full-time nanny in the office, something I could not afford. It seemed that there were no professional women in the same situation as me.

Everyone has different circumstances when embarking on parenthood. We had just bought our first house and some repairs and improvements were underway. These were still ongoing when my son arrived. We didn't have much in the way of savings after the expense of building works. Like most people of our generation, we needed two salaries to pay the mortgage. We are used to living frugally; we share one car. We would not have been able to get by on one salary plus maternity pay for a year. Notwithstanding, I had a business which, with a young team, still needed me to run it. I couldn't just take six months or more off. Thankfully, my husband managed to negotiate part-time work for the first five months of our son's life. This meant we could share a lot of the responsibility.

In the past the role of looking after a baby has been much belittled. It isn't seen as important or as hard as a job. And, of course, it is a responsibility that generally falls to women who make the corresponding sacrifice to their careers. I think the only people who truly believe this now are those who have never had full-time responsibility of children for any period of time.

FIGURE 9.1 Making calls while pushing the pram

MONTH BY MONTH: WHAT IS POSSIBLE

Below is my account of the first year of my son's life, while running my architecture practice: the good and the bad. This is what I wanted to read when I was a new parent. One of the best pieces of advice I was given prior to having a baby was that, despite the sleep deprivation, hard work and lack of control over your life, if you really want to make something happen, you can. When I was sitting in toilets expressing milk between meetings, that rang through my ears. I really wanted this to work, so it did.

The following is going to read as though my only concern was about getting work done. It wasn't at all, but this is how I did get work done. Presumably that is why you are reading this bit, not to hear me coo over how lovely my son was (there's plenty of that, elsewhere).

I have split this up into chronological order because babies change so quickly in the first year and this affects how you can work around them. It will also be a bit different for every baby. I was fortunate in that Felix did not have any illnesses and slept well during the night (not so, during the day).

Pre-baby preparation and shock

Before I found out I was pregnant, I was working full-time. I decided to see if I could manage to keep my business running and still earn enough when I was part-time. I worked with a business coach to create a 90-day plan to help me with this. I also used the help of my regular women's coaching group. I delegated as much as I could, created more systems and trained my team to win jobs without me. I used my 'spare' time for writing, to ensure that I kept it free. It worked. Not only did I get pregnant, but also I had almost halved my hours.

I had a bit of a shock when my baby bump started showing. It put potential clients off working with me. Not all, but enough to reduce my sales conversion percentage by half. I even took to taking half my team with me on sales visits so that it drilled home the fact that the business was not all about me. I had not expected this, and so it made me very cautious of telling anyone that I had a newborn at home. It also made me extra careful about phone calls being quiet. I even blamed my son's screaming on the neighbours' children once! From a feminist point of view, it seemed unfair that my sales were being damaged by being visibly pregnant, something a man would not need to worry about.

On the whole, most of my clients had no concerns. However, I was fully aware of the contrast of trying to create a professional environment from a home that was dominated by a tiny human. I felt under pressure to maintain a business-like image.

Once a baby arrives, the ability to have a train of thought that reaches a conclusion is rarely possible. At first, I was completely exasperated, but quite soon I developed some strategies for coping. Here they are.

One Week Old

I did not work for the first three weeks. I wouldn't recommend that anyone does for the first two months or more, if possible. I did not have the wonderful euphoria that some mothers experience. I imagine this is nature's way of helping you cope with those first two weeks. I kept reading online about how things would improve by three months. That felt like years away. Looking back, those first two to three months did pass very slowly. After that it sped away. Now I look back with rose-tinted glasses, because despite it being hell on earth to have so little sleep and a screaming infant (a two-minute stressful shower was all I managed all day and my only escape from the sofa and feeding), babies are magical. It's an incredibly powerful time. It is really worth keeping a diary, because you forget everything so quickly and the reality of that time is often far different from your memory of it.

Three Week Old: Office Meeting

Initially, office meetings were held in my home. The first one was when my baby was three weeks old. My husband was on hand to make tea and help if needed. Generally, Felix sat on my lap, fed or slept in his Moses basket. I was very apprehensive about the first meeting (I never did manage to feel comfortable breastfeeding in front of others). Babies are so unpredictable; I couldn't be sure what would happen. I felt quite helpless. Because I had a baby on my lap, I had to ask others to pass me things and take control sometimes. It is totally daft to say this, but I felt a bit silly.

I had quite a big battle with the midwifes about that first office meeting. They wanted to come and weigh Felix. I said that they couldn't come that day because I had an office meeting. I found it very stressful to have more than one event in the day with a baby to look after as well. They questioned what I would do with Felix during that time, as if I would just abandon him in a corner and forget about him. I felt as if they were judging me: 'Oh, here is another woman who is putting her career before her baby,' but that was so far from the truth. I had to tackle old-fashioned mindsets towards my (modern) way of working at every step. It was hard enough being a new parent, without having to do that as well. However, they did come around to my situation eventually and were a great support after this.

One Month: Office Meeting in Oxford

When he was one month old, I took my son on the train, in the sling to our usual meetings café in Oxford. I was quite stressed out beforehand. I didn't know if he would like the train journey, I didn't know if he would scream all the way through the meeting, I didn't know if I would accidentally flash everyone while breastfeeding (I was still learning how to do this!), I didn't know if he would have a poo explosion. This is why people don't generally take babies to business meetings. Babies are not very professional!

The image of the carefree mother, baby in sling, wandering about (usually in nature) was the complete opposite of how I felt. It was hot and heavy. On my trips into Oxford, I looked longingly at everyone else who was not carrying a baby. How free they looked! Some of them appeared to be having a lunch break – A LUNCH BREAK!!!!???

In reality, I needn't have worried. He gained a reputation in the café as being a baby that never cried (not true). He really enjoyed looking at everyone. Most of the time, he was happy playing with a spoon.

However, I did have some mini disasters. There was one time when I visited a potential client who was interested in a Passivhaus. She wanted to see me urgently and couldn't wait for a time when I would be baby-free. My business was struggling with a lack of new enquiries at this point, so delaying it wasn't an option. The meeting went well enough. I took a colleague who filled in when I needed to dash out to feed him. On the way back after the meeting, while waiting at the bus stop, he weed down my leg. In some ways, it was a relief that a worst-case scenario had actually happened.

If I were doing it all again, I would only schedule-in meetings when I could be baby-free. I just can't be my full professional self with a baby strapped to me. Existing clients were fine and some of them were very keen to meet him. It was easy to tell when it was appropriate to take him.

0–2 months: Tools to help the sling, Pram and the car

This is the time of the most sleep deprivation because a baby needs feeding every two to three hours. I was exhausted and bored at the same time. So work was a useful escape from that.

It felt like I was sitting on the sofa, feeding the baby all the time – but I had one hand free. I could position a chair in front of the sofa and put a laptop on it. I could type one-handed, watch videos for research, read blogs, I could sketch my ideas and upload them to my team on Slack. My colleagues commented that I was actually more on hand than usual in that way. Later on, when he got bigger, a carefully positioned cushion gave me two free hands!

FIGURE 9.2 Working one-handed while breastfeeding

Slack kept me in touch with the working world, which was very important to me. My whole world

FIGURE 9.3 Working around a baby in a sling

had been turned upside down by this new tiny human, but the working world had not changed. I was still an architect and businesswoman. I could still do that. However, I was never sure if I was getting the baby thing right.

I found that I could make phone calls while pushing the pram or while walking in the sling. This was the only way to guarantee some quiet.

My son was not good at napping in the day, but the buzz of a café seemed to soothe him for longer. Working around a baby in a sling is difficult. It's also hot and uncomfortable (possibly less so for those with smaller babies), but you can sketch, write notes, talk on the phone, read emails, listen to a business podcast. Eat a meal in peace.

Childcare at this time (for the first five months) was only a block of a maximum of two hours and carried out by my husband on his days off (two days a week). This was to fit in around feeding time. I also organised phone call meetings at 5pm when he got home from work. It was tough on both of us, but we got through it.

Later on, we could ask grandparents, which provided some additional help, but this was still limited to two or three hours due to feeding times. This and childcare generally increased as I dropped one feed at a time from seven months onwards. However, this is hugely variable on the mother and child.

Using the car as an office was also helpful. While my husband drove us to Wales to visit relatives, I worked on my laptop. I am fortunate not to suffer from travel sickness.

First Three Months (Or More): Getting More Sleep

There is a reason why sleep deprivation and the sound of children crying are used as torture techniques. I was aware of how lack of sleep can impact decision-making. I couldn't let lack of sleep create problems for my clients or business.

A helpful midwife suggested that my husband could do one feed (around 10.30pm until midnight) with a bottle, which would enable me to sleep for five hours in one go, which made a big difference. I would use that system again.

For the first three months, Felix slept downstairs in a Moses basket and we took shifts on the sofa next to him, so that whoever was sleeping was not interrupted by baby crying. This really helped, but we were like passing ships.

Anytime: More Time-saving tips

I hesitate to include an 'organisation' tip here, because I know that I am probably preaching to the converted and this could be patronising, but I found it really useful (still do) to group tasks into short, admin-type tasks and longer tasks that needed intense concentration. I would fit in the small tasks during breastfeeding or while waiting for dinner to cook. The longer tasks were booked in for when I had childcare or for when Felix did have a nap during the day. To make the most of these precious childcare sessions, I would prepare and plan while breastfeeding. I didn't need to waste childcare time with decision-making on what needed doing. Tim Ferriss has written about block-booking activities of the same type to save time. I regularly do this with phone calls and emails. I also write a separate list of 'decisions' on my to-do list. This helps me to understand what is holding me back from completing the task. I know I need to book in some thinking time or work out what information I need to help me with that decision. Often, part of this can be delegated to others. Thinking time is easy to incorporate into baby-sling walking.

I don't receive any notifications on my phone apart from missed phone calls. I have to manually go into an app to check messages. Mostly, my phone is on silent. This stops me being interrupted. Something that is even more stressful since I had a child!

As described in previous chapters, Cal Newport has written an excellent book called *Deep Work*, which goes into more of these themes on separating work types.

HAVING IT ALL IS UTTER B****KS

Before I had Felix, I was under no illusion that being a parent would look like an Instagram post. I knew it would be messy and exhausting and that I was about to embark on the biggest challenge (and it was), but nothing prepared me for the shock of the impact that Felix had on my life. I spend a lot of time working in cafés. From the next table, it used to look like parents (and it's usually mums) were having a lot of fun. The babies looked cute, the mums looked happy. It was all hunky-dory. I now notice the frequent crying and haggard looks of most mums. In café situations, I was permanently on edge with my newborn.

FIGURE 9.4 Some of the team and baby bump on site (my blue hi-vis is no longer compliant)

There is no question that when you have a baby, you have to give up other things to allow room for it to take over your life. I am someone who has many hobbies. In the first three months, I gave up everything apart from the bare necessity. Life was just one long rolling feeding/sleeping/working/nappy-changing cycle with very little variation. That is hard. Without a nanny/housekeeper and if you are working too, there is no time to get your 'body back' as so many media posts harp on about. I needed coffee, cake and beer to get me through that time.

Finally, some celebrity women are being more truthful about how much help they have. With more paid-for help, I would have had time to post about how great 'having it all' was as well.

I had huge guilt about asking for any kind of help with raising my own child. It felt like I was letting Felix down or abandoning him. I felt like I wasn't good enough. I should be able to look after my own child on my own. I read that in the past, babies were often left with grandparents during the day, so that the younger, fitter parents could work in the fields. This is in our DNA. It's only society and work pressures that has kept families apart and unable to help as much. It really does take a village to raise a child. I felt less guilty after reading these things. I hope you will too.

A priority for me was my allotment. It's an essential part of my mental health. In the first year, I grew about half the usual amount. I focused on just spending time there, growing things I really loved. I did this by timing naps with allotment time at the weekends. Felix slept under the oak tree in summer. In cooler weather, I could drive the car right in and park next to my allotment with him sleeping inside. It was heavenly.

I am usually quite a brave person, but the fear of breastfeeding in public or of Felix crying loudly in a café prevented me from doing a lot of things. It was much easier just to stay at home. I can see why loneliness is a big problem for mothers. I missed company. Online communities helped, but it's not the same as real people.

Because of working, I didn't attend any baby groups, but I don't enjoy singing baby songs; they make me cringe. I enjoyed monthly NCT group chats. I would have liked to have more time to take Felix swimming. It is all a big compromise.

Baby brain – nah. Tired – yes. Lost your brain somewhere – no

I did find it quite tiresome when people mentioned baby brain. I know it's real for other mothers but I found that I was as sharp as I have ever been. I still made good decisions. I was still able to carry out my work to a high level. I did miss some things that I would usually pick up, but pre-baby, detail was never my strength. I have since created even better checklists! Sticking to your strengths and getting help with the other stuff is even more vital when you are this exhausted!

CONCLUSION

There is no doubt that my ability to do most of my work from home made a huge difference. Once it was feasible to do so (after three months), I prioritised things that benefit my sanity, such as allotment time and swimming. Staying mentally strong is the most helpful thing you can do during this time (or anytime!). It's crucial to business strength too.

If I were to do this again, I would definitely delegate more than I did. I was still responsible for far too many 'hats'. I was still finance, marketing, sales and architecture director as well as website tech. That's more than enough for me now, let alone with a newborn to keep alive. I would build up cash reserves. I would put someone else in charge of invoicing and project management. In Kate Northrup's *Do Less*, she describes how she whittled down her time to only the things that were her strengths (primarily marketing activities). Despite her hours going down, the business income went up. So, it is do-able, but delegation is key.

BEYOND THE BABY, WORK/LIFE BALANCE

Combining work and family life with two working parents

There is no question that this is an ongoing challenge. Children's lives change quickly and you have to adapt your working life around them. Being a working parent is HARD.

I still make time for exercise and hobbies outside of parenting and work. Some might call that selfish, but I call it survival. None of these things take up that much time, in themselves, yet they feed a constant wheel of creativity and happiness. They feed my soul. They feed my ideas at work. They make me a happier wife and parent. There is no question that they improve the quality of my work output.

In my son's first year, I allowed myself to work in quite an unhealthy way. I worked when he was awake and when he was asleep. I would not normally recommend drawing up surveys at 5am, breastfeeding with one hand and computer mouse in the other, but it worked well for me at that particular stage of my son's life. Later, it did mean that I had to slowly divorce myself from the blended 24-hour work and life cycle that I was used to. Long-term, it's an unhealthy way to be.

Both of us parents are exhausted after a day at work and find it hard to switch to full-on childcare in the afternoons and evenings. Toddlers are especially high energy. They won't let you just flop in front of the TV!

Because we shared the responsibility of parenting in those early years, my husband didn't come home wondering why the house was messy or the washing-up hadn't been done. He got it. He knew first-hand how hard it could be. This reduced the pressure considerably.

WORKING WITH SPOUSE

My husband and I now work together some of the time. I always thought it would be a bad idea to work with your spouse, but it has been an improvement to our work/life balance. James is undertaking a career change and training part-time at university to become an architectural technologist. He helps the company with surveys and building control drawings around his studies. We have different strengths and don't compete with each other. We know what each of our roles are. This is key to our thus far harmonious relationship. That's not to say there hasn't been some friction! We have had to create some ground rules, such as not talking about work in the evenings. I work quite intensely and dislike being interrupted. Though awkward to begin with, we now book in time for questions and sharing ideas. Flexible working is helpfully shared with him; we can be spontaneous and go off for picnics or a day trip if we want to. It

FIGURE 9.5 My allotment shed is often where I write books or marketing material; it helps me to separate different parts of my job and it is a wonderful creative space

is really useful that we can share the responsibilities of picking up from the childminder and parenting generally.

SEPARATING WORK AND HOME LIFE WHEN YOU WORK FROM HOME

When working from home, the boundaries between work and home can feel very blurred. The important thing is to recognise when this happens and to keep pulling yourself back into good practice.

Tools that I have found to work well for me are:

- Starting the working day with a walk, listening to a podcast. I always come back feeling better and looking forward to my first coffee. If my son is at nursery, I will work from home. If not, I will head out to a coffee shop or co-working space to work. Coming home for lunch is a nice break when I do this.
- I know that ideally you should either meditate or walk mindfully in the mornings, but I often find my brain fills with my to-do list. An upbeat podcast is a great distraction and I do notice the trees and the sky more.

- I structure my day to give me a routine and also to make me more productive. My focus is really good between 8am and lunchtime. I have a post-lunch dip which is good for basic admin, going for a walk or chopping vegetables. I don't really pick up again focus-wise until after 4pm. So, afternoons are a good time to have meetings. Famous artists and writers used to spend time in the afternoons with friends or walking, so if it's good enough for them... Since I have consistently booked in client meetings in the afternoon, I have felt much less stressed. This is because I haven't lost crucial focus time in the morning. Meetings are a time-sink. It's useful to schedule them when you lose the least.
- I view exercise and allotment time as a creativity break. By calling it that, it reminds me how helpful it is to my workflow and that it isn't just about me taking time out. It also enables better thinking
- If I can, I like to go for another walk or tend the garden in the evening, as this helps me to take a mental break. These days I often prepare slow-cooker meals in the morning or during my lunch break so I am not panicking about what to cook for dinner during a time when I am trying to complete a piece of work or walking. Sometimes my walk highlights something I have forgotten, so I often attend to that before we eat as a family. After this I am mostly tied up with family activities, with the occasional book club and yoga class thrown in.
- I like to get away from the house and visit family at the weekend, take my son swimming or to a park and head to my allotment on Sunday mornings. We also like visiting gardens as a family. These activities are very restorative and help me forget about work.
- Investing in regular business coaching, personal development and hypnotherapy has given me many tools to cope with stressful times. I still need to remind myself to do this often. When I let it slip, I soon regret it!
- Don't leave important or difficult jobs to Friday. Tackle them on Monday or Tuesday. Then you won't get stressed out on a Friday because you need some help, but the person who could help you has already gone home for the weekend. It also makes your week get gradually easier, instead of gradually harder. That is much nicer.

CHAPTER 10

Case Studies

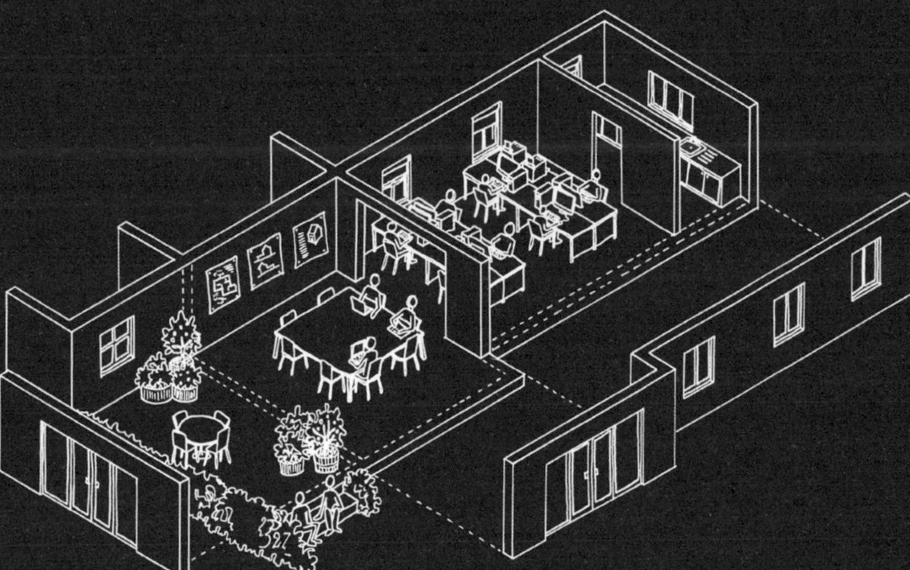

INTRODUCTION

I chose these case studies to highlight how innovative architects can be in business. There is a proactive approach shared by all the small practices in this book. They vary in size from one- to eight-people firms. All of them have a vision and have applied it in different ways to bring in the work they want. Many have opted for diversification, exploring sideline interests that support their architectural work. Three run social enterprises. Others want to make better design accessible to all (without making themselves poor in the process, a trap I fell into!). A few collaborate, accessing larger projects (even internationally) but retaining the agility of a small practice or a company of one. One practice has developed an app, another a publishing arm. All share different ways to attract the work they want, whether by suggesting sites, proposing projects that are needed or digital marketing.

FIGURE 10.1 The Office S&M team: Hugh McEwen, Catrina Stewart, Bolurin Adedipe and Abigail Yeadon

OFFICE S&M

STARTED	2013
TYPE OF WORK	domestic, commercial, public realm
SIZE	Four people, two architect partners, one PI, one PII
FOUNDERS	directors and architects Catrina Stewart and Hugh McEwen, also part founders of DAC.
LOCATION	Dalston, London

START-UP PROCESS

Initially, Stewart and McEwen worked around their day jobs. Over the years they increased their own work, firstly just a day a week, then finally losing the day jobs and combining practice with teaching. In 2019 they were turning down opportunities because they just didn't have the time to focus on them. That felt like a shame, so they decided to take the jump to full-time practice.

Now, with completed work shown on their website, clients are coming to them for their unique approach.

TYPE OF WORK

Office S&M's work strives to be joyful, investigative and inventive, specialising in materials, colour and social modes. Spotting opportunities where others see obstacles, the practice embraces projects that aren't polite. Its work is a 50/50 split between public and private, including house extensions, commercial, market refurbishments, public realm, public art and engagement projects. It tries to see the connections between all those things.

One of their first projects was Store Projects and Store School, a collective of artists, designers and writers set up in 2012. S&M was a part of it, working with 41 others right from the beginning. Its work was very varied, including a stage set, 40 videos, lots of installation projects in Bloomsbury and outside a café called Store Street Espresso. It has really developed over the years, with an after-school club and a shop in King's Cross.

FIGURE 10.2 Store Projects.

COLLABORATION

Office S&M is part of the Dalston Architecture Collective (DAC), a collaboration of 14 different practices working out of the same space in Dalston, London. They each operate as separate entities but come together for bigger projects.

Stewart says, 'the only reason that we started the company was three projects where we were collaborating with other architects. If we didn't have that, maybe we wouldn't have been able to start.'

FIGURES 10.3 AND 10.4 Finsbury Park shopfronts with Jan Kattein Architects

S&M sees collaboration as something that's very important in architectural practice. As a duo they are already collaborating, with the partnership with DAC being an extension of that and their legal structure (being an LLP) a reflection of that. Their first (and the beginning of a) longer-term collaboration began with Jan Kattein Architects. It gives them access to projects they would normally find too big. Additionally, Stewart says, the client can see that you're more of an equal to the other competitors.

COLLABORATION APPOINTMENTS

Office S&M finds that it's often easier for a council to administer a single contractual point with everyone else then being consulted to it. However, it is seeing other set-ups and there's more of a push for consortium, which can allow for more parallel contracts rather than it just being top-down.

When collaborating with Jan Kattein Architects, S&M was appointed as sub-consultants. When working with other members of DAC, it's more informal, which allows for flexibility. It feels that an umbrella company would not represent its individuality, which is a client asset. For example, Assemble works as a CIC and has certain members of the DAC team working with it on certain jobs.

CLIENT BENEFITS AND THE RISK ASSOCIATED WITH THE COLLABORATION APPROACH

Office S&M sees how collaboration benefits the client and the end users by offering something that's particular and really special. It's really positive. It also offers the client a more personal approach. Presently it is working on a project with AOC and three other architects. There are three project groups, each with its own high street. The client is offered something unusual, as each area is allotted its own specific designer. It's a way of achieving variety.

Office S&M has experienced occasional reluctance by the client to hire five different architects, requesting a lead consultant instead. Otherwise, however, the practice has received positive comments.

As Stewart says: 'Often on larger projects, [councils] have to appoint a bigger practice. But if they can appoint a few smaller practices, then they also are able to support more small businesses within the borough or within the country. I suppose it's something that all councils want to do and want to be seen to do. It's always the same names that you see winning competitions. It's nice to have younger and smaller companies as well.'

McEwen adds, 'By explaining that we've been working together for a number of years, and that we all occupy the same workspace, there are a number of ways in which we're almost de-risking the process for them. It's a tested forum.'

NEW DIRECTIONS

Office S&M thinks we will see more practices collaborating in the future. It is witnessing more and more larger – maybe more established – practices wanting to offer something fresh and new within competition bids, understanding how they can deliver a lot of different specialisms.

McEwen says, 'By teaming up, we can have the same amount of resource as a much larger practice. Grouping together with 14 different practices gives us a combined head count of 30 or 40 people. It provides the ability

FIGURE 10.5 Shape Newham, The Pollution Gate, with AOC and Carver Haggard

for us to offer something much more. Most of those practices have incredible experience in a whole variety of areas from Passivhaus through to massive workspace fit-outs. It's really good to be able to draw on and offer that, as packages for different jobs.'

SUPPORT

At DAC there is a communal support network via a WhatsApp group 'where you can ask people for advice, give tips or have a moan'. S&M believes that peer group is super important, because as a small practice you don't have the overarching structure of a 50- or 400-person practice. You are missing that benefit that other architects, doing similar jobs, might have.

HOPED-FOR CHANGES IN THE ARCHITECTURE INDUSTRY

Stewart would like to see more creativity, joy and variety in London. 'A lot of the new developments are all very similar, with only one material and quite beige.'

She would like to see more support for smaller practices and for councils and developers to take a little bit more design risk.

When asked about AI and robots changing the industry, McEwen takes an interest but believes that despite pre-fabrication, much work is still carried out by builders on site 'with cold-fingers', so it's best to design for that. Additionally, there's still a lot of existing building stock that needs upgrading. He believes there's a lot of opportunity to address unintelligent design in the public realm via retrofit.

FIGURE 10.6 The Harrison Stringfellow team in front of its office on Penny Lane, Liverpool

HARRISON STRINGFELLOW ARCHITECTS

STARTED	2010
TYPE OF WORK	residential, conversions, community and heritage projects
SIZE	six to eight people: two directors, three full-time architects, one full-time PII, two part-time admin/finance managers who work three days for the practice and two days on Airbnb/other initiatives
FOUNDERS	architects and directors Sarah Harrison and Su Stringfellow
LOCATION	Penny Lane, Liverpool

START-UP PROCESS

The start-up process began slowly with Sarah Harrison and Su Stringfellow having two children each in the early years. The directors are unusual in that they have known each other since primary school. Consequently, they instinctively understand each other's strengths and weaknesses. They both work three to four days a week, balanced with childcare responsibilities. Stringfellow believes that architects have a lot to offer beyond traditional skills, such as strategy, policy-making and creative thought. They have always set out to demonstrate that it is possible to run an architecture business, work for clients that align with your values and raise a family – and this has required some entrepreneurial thinking.

TYPE OF WORK

Harrison Stringfellow Architects (HAS) specialises in small residential, one-off homes, conversions of existing buildings for independents and community and heritage projects, mostly under the £5m mark.

FLEXIBLE WORKING

As a practice, there is one full day when everyone is together each week. Between them, the directors cover four out of five days, so there's only one day a week where either one or the other is not in the office.

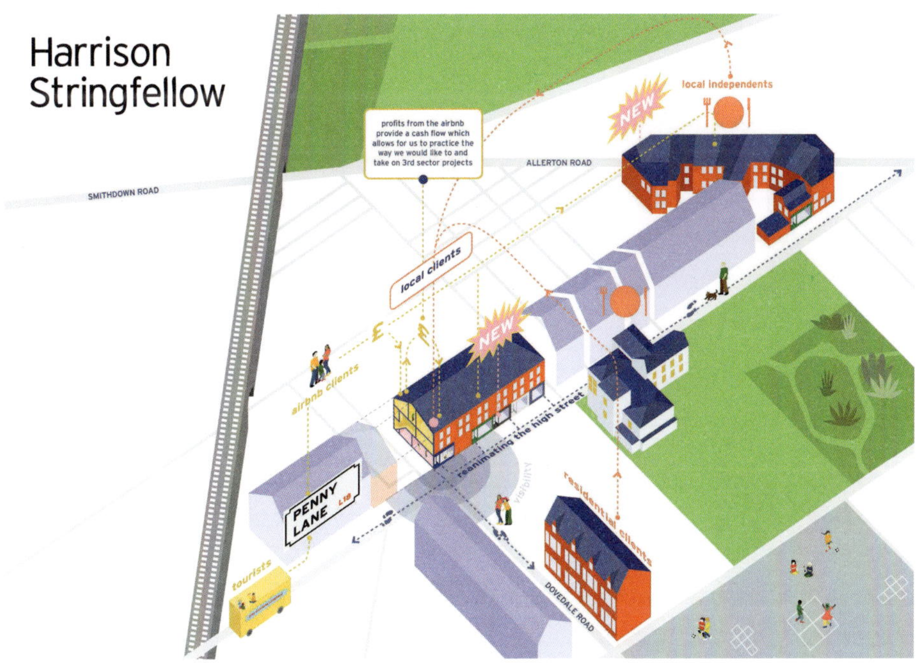

FIGURE 10.7 How diversification helps the practice to work on projects it loves

Everyone gets a look-in on all the projects. The projects tend to be planned according to each team member's skills, without pigeonholing.

ENTREPRENEURIAL

In the early days, the directors found themselves spending a lot of time entering local expressions of interest, getting to the final stage and not winning the project for various different reasons. None of these reasons made much sense, nor were they helpful to learn from. This became expensive and frustrating. They decided to spend that time and money on creating something for themselves. The investment in their office on Penny Lane was born. They rent out the upstairs space as an Airbnb, which is good for cash flow and supports the practice administrator's role.

Stringfellow was also a co-founder of Growing Sudley CIC, a social enterprise transforming a Victorian walled garden which she discovered on maternity leave. The enterprise supports vulnerable and marginalised people through nature therapy. There are a mix of paid-for and free targeted sessions, including a regular outdoor holiday club which their own children sometimes attend and which was one of the pilot projects they organised to test out the space and engage with the local community. Although the initial work was voluntary, it has now led to a fully funded capital project. The social enterprise has acquired a long lease and Power to Change funding for

FIGURE 10.8 An early concept collage for Growing Sudley CIC

FIGURE 10.9 Park Palace Ponies

a redundant council-owned building on the site. This will be converted into therapy spaces and a small community room, the income from which will keep the social enterprise running.

The experience and knowledge gained has provided other business benefits, with social enterprises approaching HSA to work with them. The practice recently won the RIBA Journal MacEwen Award for Park Palace Ponies (a social enterprise). Stringfellow says that locally social enterprises are providing support for matters that local authorities are unable to fund, especially following Covid-19. HAS's experience has brought them a lot of new work and has resulted in the employment of two new staff members, as well as aligning with its practice ethos and sustainability goals.

'We have met lots of different kinds of people, and lots of interesting things have popped up, more in line with the kind of things that we want to do,' states Stringfellow.

This entrepreneurialism isn't just fun, but necessary. Stringfellow doesn't think they would have been able to survive with architectural work alone.

She reports that the architecture side of the practice has only recently started paying for itself. The directors have tried different configurations of staff and alternative ways of executing projects, but (and this is a gripe Stringfellow has with architecture generally) unless you are willing to work long hours, some of which are unpaid (which they don't advocate because nurseries shut at 6pm), it is difficult to generate a profit on smaller jobs after salaries and expenses. From a business perspective, it doesn't stack up.

Stringfellow thinks that unless the profession starts to recognise how much work they get for free from the long hours culture, she doesn't think the demographics are going to change. They've stuck to their guns on fees and if people don't want to pay, they just don't do it. They feel confident in the quality of the product they offer and that their fees offer value for money. The majority of their work is through referral and repeat clients, which they feel is testament to the service they provide.

SYSTEMS

In the last two years HSA has changed the way it quotes for residential work. Visiting potential clients was sapping most of the directors' time. They now have a system that starts with a general enquiry form that any member of staff answering the phone can fill in. Then an information pack is sent out, whereby costs for different types of projects are roughly explained – for example, a typical extension. It describes what's involved, what the stages are and provides information on their approach. If the client is interested, they can come to the office for a free half-hour consultation, and during Covid-19 this was moved to Zoom, which is more efficient again. If the client wants a site visit, they are charged an hourly rate (deducted if they are appointed). This has reduced time spent winning work as well as knowing these clients share their values from the outset.

HSA also uses a jobs board, visible to all in the office. There they schedule out each live project and update weekly transferring to individual tasks per staff member: 'It always goes wrong, but we try!' This was particularly useful during the pandemic, as the practice was able to take this simple version to the next level and is trialling different project management software online in a collaborative manner with staff. It has started to help with efficiency and also frees up the directors from always being a funnel.

CLIENTS AND FLEXIBLE WORKING

Stringfellow says that clients have never had an issue with their flexible working policy. They have an office WhatsApp group. Clients soon get the hang of when they are around, and for some clients their evening slots (around childcare) are more convenient. She wouldn't be fazed by a large development that required daily site management, as 'we would just resource accordingly'. This is perhaps a benefit that they realised during the Covid-19 pandemic, as working from home, whilst challenging with children, became fairly seamless for all the staff who were used to communicating with the directors remotely for some of the week in any case.

NEW DIRECTIONS

HSA would love to work on a social housing scheme, demonstrating good practice. However, finding a site and how to go about it is tricky. They are still working out who to talk to. Without a wealthy family background, architects need to find other ways to fund projects. Stringfellow finds ideas

FIGURE 10.10 A Harrison Stringfellow shopfront

(like investing in their office and Airbnb on Penny Lane) just pop up when you least expect them to, 'if you go looking for them, they're never there'.

A KIND OF ONE-STOP SHOP FOR RESIDENTIAL CLIENTS

There are two reasons why HSA takes on the small residential projects, Stringfellow's partner, Mel, is a builder, and he carried out the fit-out in their office. Some of their clients are second-time round with a house project and appreciate the benefit of using a good builder. So instead of a full tender, they ask a quantity surveyor (QS) to price it. Mel then does all the work open book (the contractor is paid based on transparent costs accrued for labour and materials) and HSA charges an hourly rate to project manage it. All the budgeting is done in line with the QS's budget, open book. The practice always has a queue of home projects wanting to work in this way and it collects the data from each one in order to continually improve the accuracy on pricing. It is also a useful way of training less experienced members of staff in site-running. There's room to learn if they don't provide quite the right information, because there's no contractual relationship and Mel is working with them to make sure that problems are identified and resolved at an early stage.

In Liverpool there are often limited budgets due to house value. On more straightforward projects, HSA gives the option to the client to work with it up to contractor appointment and then the client continues with a simple householder contract without consultant.

HOPED-FOR CHANGES IN THE ARCHITECTURE INDUSTRY

Stringfellow has been disappointed by the quality of housing projects in Liverpool and hopes this might change in the future. She thinks architects could do more to promote the benefits that they can bring, and believes she could apply many skills learnt from architecture within other industries. She enjoys connecting people and projects to solve a problem. The practice is keen to provide bolt-on services, such as conservation and Passivhaus, and is training accordingly.

FIGURE 10.11 Piers Taylor in his self-built studio

INVISIBLE STUDIO

STARTED	2010
TYPE OF WORK	residential, public
SIZE	one person; works with freelancers and collaborates with other practices
FOUNDERS	architect Piers Taylor, previously a director at Mitchell Taylor Workshop, who was taught in Australia by Glenn Murcutt, an inspiration for his work today
LOCATION	near Bath

START-UP PROCESS

Piers Taylor's business model came out of the last recession. Overnight, in 2008 while at Mitchell Taylor, he found himself laying-off people and not earning a living. He states, 'As architects we're absolutely linked to frontline economic issues on so many levels.' At this time one couldn't borrow (due to the banking crisis), as there was simply no money to pay others. With three dependent children, he realised that he didn't want to be so 'beholden to the market in that manner'.

Even with a practice of 14 people, despite working on medium-sized projects and winning awards, he couldn't support his family. Moving forwards, Taylor wanted autonomy and flexibility which would allow him to spend more time with his children. He found traditional practice too restrictive for that. He was clear that he wanted fewer overheads but otherwise was not too sure of his next steps. Initially, he rented an office from a neighbour. He paid people, either task-led or more collaboratively. Having lost a lot of money with Mitchell Taylor, it was very important for him to know his costs upfront. If he won a fee for a piece of work of £7,000, he could outsource £2,000 of that to relieve him of a chunk of it. It gave him much more control. When he got busier, he started paying an hourly rate to people he knew from Mitchell Taylor and from his children's school.

TYPE OF WORK

When Invisible Studio began (around 10 years ago), Taylor was working on quite small projects that 'only just washed their faces' when paying someone an hourly rate. Freelancers' hourly rates need to be quite high to cover their own overheads (software, office, etc). For a while Taylor trialled employing

FIGURE 10.12 Invisible Studio

FIGURE 10.13 Indiana Farmhouse

somebody but his employee wanted security and a future, which Taylor couldn't offer. Having been bruised during the previous recession, he didn't want the additional responsibility of securing work for others. Taylor now takes on bigger projects, which is much better for him because the fee is more generous, leaving more room for experiment. He's careful to pitch well.

Taylor had a long-term working relationship with a former director of FCB Studios. Now a freelancer, Tara Breen delivers all Invisible Studio projects on an hourly rate. Taylor estimates Breen's salary at £65,000, which is much more than he would ordinarily pay a project architect. However, as an architect of the same age, he's an incredibly experienced job runner, putting together packages of working drawings and completely dependable. Taylor loves not having to organise his time. 'If we have a lull, he'll go do something else, but generally I've kept him very busy for four years.'

With him and the FCB Studios-related network that came with him, Taylor has been able to take on much bigger projects, up to £7 million. Some of this network live abroad; for example in Berlin. Having come out of the same studio (FCB), they all use the same drawing packages as everyone else. Although 70% of Invisible Studio work is carried out on this hourly rate model, Taylor recognises the risk. The freelancers could all disappear tomorrow. However, having known them all for a long time, there is considerable trust and his clients like them a lot. You can imagine that there is a mutual benefit for them to work on interesting projects with Taylor. In practical terms, they all have Invisible Studio addresses, as well as addresses for the other firms they might work for.

FIGURE 10.14 Collaborating in the woodshed

COLLABORATION

'I found the most stressful thing in the whole of my time and architecture has been not being able to resource a project properly. I only take on projects now that I know I can resource. And what that means is, how I do pay people an hourly rate?'

Collaboration works both ways, of course. When Kate Darby, an architect Taylor has known for a long time, was not busy and could spare an employee, he hired Gemma Wheeler from her studio to do a piece of work, with an allowance for studio running costs on top. This system can also increase locational viability of projects. Taylor worked with Darby on a church project. They split the fee, but Darby could attend all the site meetings, as her practice was situated closer to the site.

Taylor has worked with Meredith Bowles of Mole Architects on a Forest School camp project in the Fens. It was quite low fee but worked because Bowles is very local. Taylor and Bowles have been appointed as the lead architects but in collaboration (the PI insurance is combined). File share, including timesheets, are on Dropbox.

With Charley Brentnall's organisation, Carpenter Oak, Invisible Studio has recently won another project at Westonbirt, on a design build contract. The client is completely open to this sort of collaboration; they just apportion the fee accordingly.

Taylor pays a variety of people for specific chunks of work, from students for physical or sketch-up models to James Eagle (a UK architect living in Greece) with quite a low fee of £125/day on V Ray, Rhino modelling and

FIGURE 10.15 Hadspen Apiary

rendering. Taylor is finding that with the bigger fees he has more confidence outsourcing sections of the work. A domestic extension only needs to run over by a week and money has been lost. Taylor realises that less experienced and therefore cheaper people can produce a working drawings package, but more experienced people can do them quickly and with less management.

Taylor himself works on projects at different stages. He carries out a lot of site visits. He has described to me in the past how much he enjoys conveying a lot of information in a single sketch, and it saves time, especially on site. He also works with executive architects (usually larger firms that deliver the project). Invisible Studio takes it up to planning and then charges a smaller handover fee. This has enabled Taylor to work on Indiana Farmhouse, a project in America.

SAFETY IN DIVERSIFICATION

Taylor pessimistically often expects not to win another project. He was bitten hard by the uncertainty in the last recession and so chooses to diversify, which he does via TV presenting, a PhD, small writing projects and teaching. The theory behind this is that one does not depend on the other, though they are all related and complementary. He is also working on building an Airbnb in the woods where he is based.

VALUE OF ARCHITECTS

'I think the really interesting thing about architects and why we're different from technicians, is that we do many different things and our skills are juggling the complexities and making it work. Even just getting planning [permission] is a complex thing, we have to juggle multiple stakeholders, legal issues, contractual issues and architectural issues, spatial issues, design issues, client issues, people management issues. Technicians focus on the technical issues, [but architects] are trained to deal with multiple issues and that's [part] of our business model.'

NEW DIRECTIONS

Taylor wants to continue working on interesting buildings and making a difference. Having worked on a PhD, he can see the links between it and practice, finding opportunities for an overlap where research can be done in an academic sense alongside practice. He wants to bring more practice into his teaching, getting students to work on live projects. After all, 90% of what we know about architecture comes from practical experience; working with a client who has a different value system from ours as architects, things that architecture school does not teach you. It's really important for Taylor that he can make a living from architecture, a living that feels good, notwithstanding in the context of the length and cost of training. He loves the autonomy over his own time, knowing that he can collect his children from school without any questions being asked or that he can pop out to tinker on something for a brain break.

HOPED-FOR CHANGES IN THE ARCHITECTURE INDUSTRY

Taylor describes the difficulty in winning public work, and why one would want to do it for only a 2% fee. Consequently, he finds the quality of railway stations, hospitals and schools quite miserable now. He recommends the book *Why Architects Matter: Evidencing and Communicating the Value of Architects* by Flora Samuel.

Taylor would like to see us get much better at explaining what we do, why we are needed. We can't think of ourselves as 'the hero' anymore – that has nothing to do with what the client values most. We need to be working with housebuilders, contractors and government, and really making a difference. Taylor himself worked in local government in the early days, as he wanted to find out how it works. Clients have to take a lot of risk when buying a site in this country, as there is no certainty in what might be allowed with planning restrictions. In other countries you buy a plot knowing more or less what you can build there.

FIGURE 10.16 AND 10.17 Indiana Farmhouse at night. Indiana Farmhouse in winter.

AI AND ROBOTS

Piers recommends *The Reflective Practitioner: How Professionals Think in Action* by Donald Schön.

'It makes it so clear about the type of skill that we need to judge situations between the lines with our clients, students and contractors. It's so subtle, the difference between a good building and a bad building, the difference between a good relationship with the client and a bad relationship, and I feel we're constantly juggling all those things. 90% of architecture is people telling you that you can't do something. You can't build that, you can't get consent, you can't put a window there. I think that's our core skill, not a technical act of making something and keeping the rain out, it's pushing aside all of those competing issues that want to stop a project.'

FIGURE 10.18 Transition by Design team: Charlie, Andy, Alex, Wongani, Niki, Kate and Katie (Lucy is not pictured)

TRANSITION BY DESIGN

STARTED	2013 (having worked together since 2011)
TYPE OF WORK	green architecture/retrofit, domestic, research
SIZE	eight people: three architects, one architectural designer, three research and project designers, one studio manager
FOUNDERS	directors Alex Towler and Andy Edwards
LOCATION	Oxford

FIGURE 10.19 Manor Farm

Transition by Design (TbD) is now a cooperative. It has open and voluntary membership, and decision-making is carried out by members. After one year of working with the practice, membership of the co-op can be applied for.

START-UP PROCESS

TbD's directors, Alex Towler and Andy Edwards, started working out of their homes and coffee shops, and then progressed to sharing space with other like-minded companies. When they were given short notice to leave an office space, they created Makespace, using an empty, university-owned building in Oxford for start-ups with ethical aims.

TYPE OF WORK

Their work comprises three strands – green architecture and retrofit (such as Manor Farm, Figure 10.19), community-led housing projects (such as the Thame Community Land Trust, Figure 10.21) and research (such as the 'homemaker' project, where they work with people in acute housing needs). The research projects involve running events to raise awareness, finding stakeholders and working out what points they could piggy-back off other projects. Through this research TbD has been able to identify one of the biggest critical issues within the housing crisis in Oxford: move-on accommodation. Research projects have led to multiple collaboration, such as the new Oxford Rough Sleeper and Assessment Hub (see Figure 10.22). There's a nice synergy between all of it – what can be achieved as a whole or a collective is far greater than one single practice.

COLLABORATION

As well as a community interest company, TbD is a non-profit company which helps to attract research grants and funding (some grant streams are not open to profit-making companies). Functionally, this means the company can't pay dividends. The community-funded projects can operate in different ways, so TbD can use the money itself for events or research, or a community organisation can access the money and employ the practice in a traditional way, as architects.

Working together in a cooperative structure means that members take on tough decisions as a whole. You share in both the difficult times and the great times. There are a lot of benefits, but it can be challenging to adjust. A new member can arrive with norms that came from hierarchical practice. There needs to be a dialogue to set expectations. It has benefits as a kind of safety net for practice values. Socially or environmentally detrimental projects will just not pass through the net. All members work flexibly, some work part-time, and this requires trust and flexibility on both sides. Because its non-hierarchical, members don't report only to one person; it's much more circular. They use digital tools such as Slack and Notion for project management. This flexibility and digital savvy helped TbD a lot during the Covid-19 lockdown.

NEW DIRECTIONS

TbD is not interested in growth for its own sake but would like to work on larger city-wide projects to enable greater change. It is currently working with the covered market in Oxford. Housing is a growing specialism and it would like to continue with more community-led projects. Though not

FIGURE 10.20 Open House, Oxford

FIGURE 10.21 Thame Community Land Trust

particularly profitable, green retrofit is really important for the climate crisis, so TbD will continue to use its expertise on those. It also wants to further develop the research side of the practice.

HOPED-FOR CHANGES IN THE ARCHITECTURE INDUSTRY

TbD feels practices need to take more leadership on the climate challenge and social issues. Towler reflects on the era when Foster and Rogers set up their practices – they were the outliers, running private practices at a time when the majority of architects worked for the state. We are now seeing an evolution of this trend. Now, with organisations such as Public Practice, we are trying to get more architects back into councils, to make changes from within. The industry needs to get back to the essence of who we are serving. Recent events have highlighted the needs of the average citizen. Architecture and decision-making needs to change to reflect that.

FIGURE 10.22 Oxford Rough Sleeper Hub entrance

FIGURE 10.23 Gbolade directors Tara Gbolade and Seun Lanre Gbolade

GBOLADE DESIGN STUDIO

STARTED	2018
TYPE OF WORK	residential and mixed-use developments
SIZE	six people: two founders, one architect, one architectural assistant, one studio manager, one accountant
FOUNDERS	Tara Gbolade and Seun Lanre Gbolade
LOCATION	London

FIGURE 10.24 Littlehampton scheme

Gbolade is a very new practice, having started approximately three years ago. It works on residential and mixed-use developments using experience gained from previous employment. Tara Gbolade is an architect with a big vision. If I were starting again, I would follow her process to the letter! During our interview I viewed her overall plan at the beginning. It is striking how many of those things Gbolade Design Studio have achieved and more!

START-UP PROCESS

After a couple of years of starting practice focusing on residential developments, Tara Gbolade listened to the keynote speech given by Sadie Morgan at the RIBA's Guerrilla Tactics conference and applied for a place at Public Practice, a social enterprise started by Pooja Agrawal and Finn Williams, who offer built environment practitioners an alternative route into working for the public sector through influential placements within forward-thinking local authorities. There was a matching process, and Harlow and Gilston Garden Town was looking for a sustainability lead. It gave Tara an opportunity to shape the role at a time when the response to sustainability was growing, as many local authorities had recently declared a climate emergency. The initial brief was for a sustainability checklist, but Gbolade expanded the brief beyond environmental sustainability to include socio-economic sustainability as well. The eventual sustainability guidance and checklist would be used to assess incoming planning applications for the over 23,000 new homes across strategic sites in the garden town. After a 12-month placement, she was asked to stay on and then Epping Forest Council asked her to do the same, expanding the application to minor developments and refurbishments too.

Following this success, sustainability strategy is now a major practice specialism and allows the team to work on much larger projects than a micro practice would normally be offered. Councils have declared climate emergencies and Gbolade is in demand. Following the completion of her placement, Tara now sits on the Public Practice Board as an Alumni Observer while also co-running Gbolade Design Studio.

TYPE OF WORK

Clients range from SME (small- and medium-sized) developers (such as Littlehampton and Hermitage Mews, see Figures 24-26) to local authorities and housing associations. Despite the practice's small size, it is able to work on larger scale developments and public sector projects because of its collective previous experience.

Gbolade Design Studio's mission is about 'making everyday places for people extraordinary'. Whether that looks like physical spaces in architecture and placemaking or a digital space creating apps, it doesn't really matter.

Tara brings in a specialism of sustainability from her previous work, while her partner, Seun Lanre, brings in an off-site construction specialism from his work with developers.

VISIONING AND PARTNERING

Tara is a natural visionary and reads a lot of business books. She was inspired by Adam Grant's *Originals: How Non-conformists Move the World*, about how creative ideas really happen. The strength of its vision enabled Gbolade Design Studio to be very specific about marketing and networking strategies. Rather than just accepting what came in, the practice sets out to find what it wants. It also has a unique 50/50 approach to innovative

FIGURE 10.25 Littlehampton scheme

FIGURE 10.26 Hermitage Mews

ideas beyond its usual scope – which is both innovative and brave. First, it considers new ventures in terms of its own skills – does it have the expertise to deliver at least 50% of a venture? If yes, then where can it find the other 50% in the form of consultants or research? The Part 3 (now 'architect's') app was born from this approach and the practice is now proposing app development to clients as part of a programmatic opportunity – beyond the physical building. Here are architects really embracing the digital age, applying architectural skills to other fields and benefitting clients in new ways.

Gbolade describes its vision as 'a rudder to remind us that irrespective of what's going on in the world, this is who we are, this is what we're about. And it doesn't mean it doesn't change, but it allows us to preserve our core while stimulating progress.'

The team is a combination of freelance architects and app developers, as well as other disciplines. Fee percentage shares are just agreed upfront. The belief is that this generation is far more flexible in its approach to work, so the method suits a young growing practice like Gbolade Design Studio.

NEW DIRECTIONS

Graduating in the last recession in 2008 made the Gbolades decide not to rely solely on architecture as a business model, so diversification was key to survival – exploring property developments and apps. Their overall goal is to ensure they're creating environmental and socio-economically sustainable places, digitally, physically or otherwise. 'We are really open to wherever this takes us. Our architectural backgrounds give us a great starting place – but we see this only as the jump-off point and don't wish to be anchored by this – which also gives us the opportunity to collaborate with other practices or exciting generative design studios.'

Over the coming years the practice would like to start leading larger scale projects. However, it is open to projects that meet its overall mission. It understands that many businesses die through a lack of innovation. There is no danger of that at Gbolade Studio!

HOPED-FOR CHANGES IN THE ARCHITECTURE INDUSTRY

For Gbolade it's two things – sustainability and equity. Making architecture seems like a safe space for a diverse range of people and backgrounds. She thinks there is so much talent that architecture is missing out on.

She would like to see more collaboration between small and large practices within the industry – for instance, when it comes to local authority framework bids – which can be a bit of dark art.

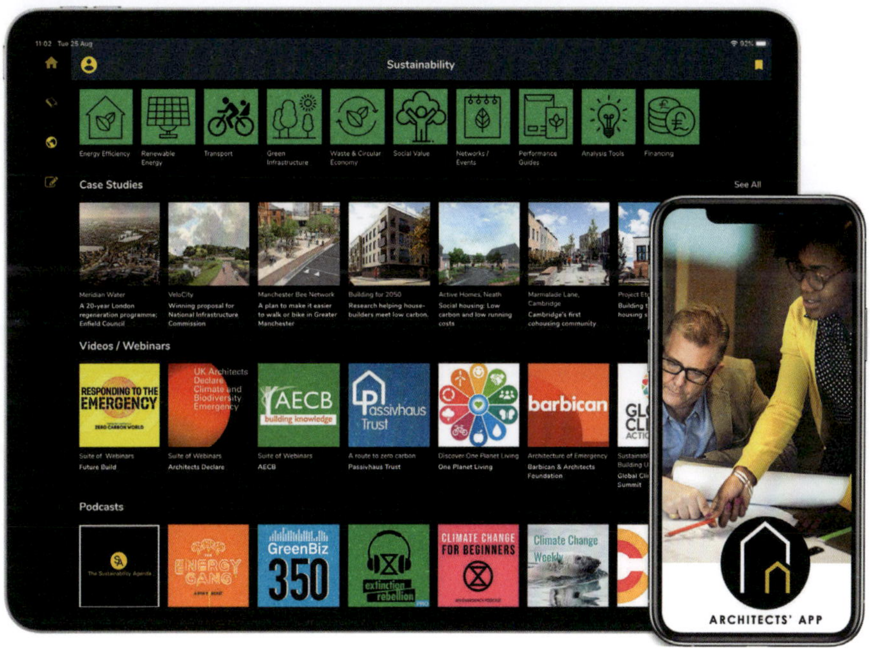

FIGURE 10.27 The architect's app

FIGURE 10.28 alma-nac directors Chris Bryant, Caspar Rodgers and Tristan Wigfall

ALMA-NAC

STARTED	2010
TYPE OF WORK	wide-ranging, including residential, education, work spaces, publishing
SIZE	eight people: three directors, one associate, one architect, two architectural assistants, one studio manager
FOUNDERS	directors and architects, Chris Bryant, Caspar Rodgers, Tristan Wigfall
LOCATION	London

START-UP PROCESS

alma-nac's first projects were unusual: a yoga studio and a snooker hall conversion into affordable housing. These projects hit some delays and the practice found itself without any income. It had already cut its ties with other paid work, so this was a tricky time. The team was young and new to architecture and didn't have established networks to fall back on. It looked at other ways of finding work and the 'Free Architecture' initiative was born. Free Architecture was a simple market stall at Portobello Market in London, offering a discussion about anything architecture-related for free. Because footfall at the market is so high, they could have a multitude of conversations about architecture with a huge array of people. This enabled them to find out a lot more about what clients want and how to approach them. It was the beginning of the practice's process-led architectural approach.

FIGURE 10.29 Dulwich Pavilion Planters – proposing new life, rather than demolition, for parts of the pavilion

TYPE OF WORK

alma-nac tries not to specialise in project type, preferring to be open to a wide range. Examples would be a 25-home apartment block, a school for 550 pupils, or a book (via their publishing arm). The practice realises you can easily get tied down to one sector, as one project will lead to another, hence its more proactive approach to finding work (see below). Despite this wide range, there is a focus on education, one-off residential (such as the House-within-a-House and Paxton House apartments, see Figures 10.31 and 10.32) and bespoke workspaces (such as the Animal Hospital, see Figure 10.30). alma-nac excels at human engagement and loves crossing over into the art world (an example could be the Dulwich Pavilion Planters, see Figure 10.29). It promotes architecture as a process rather than the final building. At the moment it is very interested in participation processes – how architecture can become more relevant to those it's being delivered to. Clients may not have found alma-nac because of its approach but they will become very interested in the benefits.

The directors enjoy connecting threads through their portfolio work. If they hadn't done project x and y, then they might have lacked the seed of an idea to go down a particular route or towards a related project.

FIGURE 10.30 Animal Hospital

FINDING WORK

alma-nac has always been very interested in proactively finding work. The team would even define entering competitions as passive. They like to propose a site, a project, an article or a book; perhaps a lesson, a display or an art show. They do this by keeping in touch with people via email, networking or writing articles that promote debate. They focus on what people want and find out more about that rather than being project-focused. This means they are not tied to one sector. Clients fall in love with them and their approach rather than on only the strength of their case studies. People buy from people after all.

WORKING TOGETHER

Starting out as three directors, alma-nac has a collaborative and non-hierarchical approach that is inclusive of newcomers. Rodgers enjoys

FIGURE 10.31 House-within-a-House

FIGURE 10.32 Paxton House

spotting individual designer identities that come through in their collective portfolio, a feature of a person that worked with them at that time. This applies to clients and consultants as well.

FREE ARCHITECTURE

For this to work, you need a high footfall, so it lends itself to urban areas. alma-nac has found it fun and liberating to keep testing, to lose the shackles of perfection in architecture school – to start a process just to see where the conversations lead. There have been other initiatives around the world, such as 50 cents architecture in Canada. The idea of 'free architecture' as a live testing operation is something that could be useful for all architecture practice.

NEW DIRECTIONS

alma-nac would like to grow, to keep doing more of the same, but it is looking forward to seeing surprises too; variations that cross-pollinate between the different streams it has. The practice intends to remain nimble and agile to allow maximum freedom in its work.

HOPED-FOR CHANGES IN THE ARCHITECTURE INDUSTRY

Rodgers paraphrases Jeremy Till, the architect, writer and educator, who has spoken of the dangers of architecture becoming a self-referential cul-de-sac. alma-nac is all about building for people rather than for itself and the practice would like to see more of this in the world.

FIGURE 10.33 Lisa Raynes, founder of Pride Road Architects

PRIDE ROAD ARCHITECTS

STARTED	2010 (as Raynes Architecture), rebranded in 2016
TYPE OF WORK	residential
SIZE	four people: three architects, one technical associate
FOUNDER	director and architect Lisa Raynes
LOCATION	nationwide, with currently three franchises

Pride Road Architects was established in 2016 as the UK's first domestic architecture franchise practice.

START-UP PROCESS

Lisa Raynes is a chartered architect with 20-plus years of experience. She started with the traditional route of going into practice and trying to work her way up, but then family came along. She found her career started plateauing and then actually nosediving. She has three children and was made redundant twice while on maternity leave at different firms. The last time was during the 2010 recession. Like me at that time, she discovered there were no jobs. Setting up on her own was the only option because she was the breadwinner.

TYPE OF WORK

Pride Road focuses on existing properties, domestic residential extensions and loft conversions valued from £20,000 to about £250,000. Initially, Raynes started working on domestic projects. Later she tried breaking into other sectors and growing the scale of projects, but soon realised the value of a niche. She has since based her success on a focused niche in the small-scale residential market.

FRANCHISE AND SYSTEMS

Today, it is a numbers game. The domestic market is very resilient and the practice works on many small projects. The benefits are not relying on one key client who could, for example, lose their funding or go insolvent. If that

FIGURE 10.34 Bungalow extension by Lisa Raynes at Pride Road Architects

FIGURE 10.35 Roof extension by Lisa Raynes at Pride Road Architects

happens you have lost a large proportion of your income. The practice risk profile is very low because the client risk is very low. It's also predictable. In terms of marketing, there is a very clear return on investment. You know how many leads you're going to generate, and the conversion rate from each lead. Raynes can set reasonable targets knowing that she needs to visit x number of clients and run x number of workshops, and then will be able to convert a certain number of projects.

The practice has set up quite sophisticated systems about the client journey. From the moment a client makes an enquiry, it keeps track of them using a CRM (customer relationship management) system. Any information it has from the client in the briefing process is retained on one record, and then as the project develops the record becomes more in-depth. From that it's really easy to pull together a pre-construction information pack, a fee proposal letter or a briefing document. Pride Road is not reinventing the wheel every time; instead the architects are spending more time doing what they love (and what they are paid for): designing and drawing.

Franchisees gain access to all these systems and business know-how for a fee. A franchisee chooses a location they want to operate in and then has the option to buy a licence to operate in that area (usually a series of postcodes that cover 70,000 owner-occupied homes within a 20-minute travel distance). The franchisee could then name itself Pride Road North

FIGURE 10.36 Lisa with franchisees Laura Simpkins and Magdalena Haener

Oxford, for example. It would be the franchisee's business, so if it were the author it might be Clare Nash Limited trading as Pride Road North Oxford. The licence lasts for five years, costing between £7,500 and £15,000. It's valuable because straightaway you would have lead-generation, a business system with proven results and support – a far cry from when I set up with no clients, no support and no idea how to run a business! Raynes recognises the most daunting thing about setting up on your own is confidence.

PROCESS

The Pride Road process is based on efficiency, which you need with high turnover of small value projects. It runs concept design workshops with clients. Once these are agreed, they pass over to a technician to draw up, overseen by the architect.

The main benefit to this type of architectural practice is that you can run it around your life and commitments rather than the other way around. You set your own appointments and schedule your working week – it is a full-time job – to suit. Because the process is so clearly defined, you are in control of your time and can plan-in other things. For example, Raynes also enjoys examining Part 3 students.

MAKING ARCHITECTURE ACCESSIBLE

Raynes is motivated by making architecture accessible to the public, making it more like something a larger brand such as John Lewis might offer, so the average mum doesn't have to go directly to the builder, she can have her extension designed properly. She's also passionate about providing opportunities for fellow architects who may have left the profession or feel overlooked in their careers or overwhelmed in their work/life balance, as are so many women architects.

NEW DIRECTIONS

Over the long term, Raynes would like to see Pride Road becoming a national contender with more franchisees.

TECHNOLOGY

Raynes is always keeping up with technology – testing if VR is a useful offering, for example. She finds we all still need that human contact with design work. So although good systems can make processes more efficient, there still needs to be a real person putting it all together. Since Covid-19, the practice has brought more technology into the client process. It pivoted online using video calling to maintain face-to-face contact where meeting in person is not possible. Freehand drawing is still the most cost-effective way to deliver concept design and Pride Road has tools to turn that into a 1:50

FIGURE 10.37 A happy family in their new kitchen

drawing. Raynes has a whole set of Lego home models that she can use to show clients different extension options (see Figure 10.38). Scale furniture can be dropped on to the drawing to help clients visualise. Using the models helps to explain to a lay person the need for structural beams, headroom for stairs and party wall issues.

HOPED-FOR CHANGES IN THE ARCHITECTURE INDUSTRY

Raynes would like to see time management taught at architecture schools. It would help to resolve the issue in architecture of over-promising and under-delivering, as well as under-valuing those working on reduced hours, due to other commitments. In a recession those people are the first to lose their jobs. It shouldn't be that way. As discussed in the rest of the book, time away from architecture can make you a better architect and brilliant at time management.

The Pride Road systems offer excellent time management templates. A briefing meeting takes 30 minutes, concept design a further two or four hours. The architect books out time in their diary to do those things in that time. The client sees the value, as you do it in front of them. As the architect you can understand what your time is worth. It's all very predictable, as the work is complete in that time. Under-valuing ourselves is the plague of the architecture industry (though I see this comes up with other business owners as well).

FIGURE 10.38 A typical Lego model

FIGURE 10.39 POoR members – Matt Harvey, Shawn Adams, Ben Spry and Larry Botchway – at Carney's Community Youth Centre, in front of a mural completed during a workshop

POOR COLLECTIVE

STARTED	2019
TYPE OF WORK	a social enterprise specialising in collaborative work with young people
SIZE	four people/partners: three architectural designers, one accountant
FOUNDERS	partners Shawn Adams, Larry Botchway, Ben Spry, Matt Harvey
LOCATION	London

START-UP PROCESS

All four member founders have full-time jobs in architecture, mostly dedicating time at the weekends and after work to get the paperwork done.

The members of POoR all have similar upbringings and backgrounds. Larry, Ben and Shawn felt a desire to not just study architecture but to have a stake in the environment, crafting a piece of their surroundings. They all embraced the social dimension of what architects can do.

As teenagers, they benefitted from youth facilities or clubs. It gave them the opportunity to meet people from their local area and see young people – probably only five or 10 years older than them – lead activities. These leaders brought in a wealth of different practitioners to teach them life skills, such as how to conduct yourself and be street smart, or how to avoid certain crimes; skills that were relevant and shaped their characters.

Over the years, they've seen the closing of these youth facilities. They've seen young people hit hard in the UK, whether it's from the price of admission to university or the cost of living. POoR wants to be able to give back, to inspire young people and be able to empower them. They felt fortunate that they were able to go to these youth clubs before they closed and gained a lot from them. The youth clubs offered a range of activities, such as performing arts, football, basketball and other creative interests that you don't necessarily get an opportunity to do in school. However, they never had an opportunity to meet an architect. That could have made a big impact on their decisions. They're trying to give young people those opportunities and show them options that they may not have thought of. When Shawn was younger, he thought you must like maths and physics to be an architect, but 'physics nearly killed me'. For him, to be able to go to schools and say, 'Hey, you don't necessarily have to study physics,' is rewarding. He can see the impact he's making when speaking with the children. Sometimes they are so pleased to receive advice, and are overwhelmed by the idea that they could also become an architect. If Shawn's art teacher hadn't suggested architecture, he might not have taken that route. These critical moments can lead to complete change.

TYPE OF WORK

POoR's vision focuses the development of communities through the elevation of young people. All the work it does has a youth-centred dimension to it, whether that's working with local communities or working directly with young people with specific barriers. At the moment, POoR's work is within London, but the members are hoping to expand, working nationally or internationally. They have been working together for over a year and they feel like they are at embryonic stage, but the world is their oyster!

FIGURE 10.40 A young person painting a mural at a workshop held at Carney's Community Youth Centre

An example project is a wall mural near Battersea, for Carney's Community Youth Centre (see Figures 10.40–10.42), which teaches young people boxing and how to fix bikes. POoR was asked to create a mural to brighten up the exterior facade, and the members were interested immediately. They decided to run a small co-design process, using their ability to think about how art and design impacts the function of a space, but also how it integrates with its community. They ran several coaching sessions with the young people there and designed using their wisdom. Larry says: 'They gave us ideas that we would have never thought of, and also rejected quite a lot of our assumptions as well.'

EMPOWERING YOUNG PEOPLE

Shawn says it was hard but they had to give up some of their design agency in order to improve the project.

As Ben states: 'The young people at Carney's understand the area better than we do, they have daily experiences that are different. The project could have been weaker if we just came in with our own assumptions. [By working in this way] you're inviting them to have a seat at the table. But it has equal merit to yours. It's a truly equal partnership. To do something like that, you don't have to be a designer.'

They don't believe you necessarily need to be a designer to run workshops like this. On one occasion, Matt (the accountant in his day job) was the only one who could make it that day to run an engagement session. He was able to run a co-design session with a group of young people because he understands how to engage with them effectively.

FIGURE 10.41 POoR members painting with young people at Carney's Community Youth Centre

WHERE DO THE OPPORTUNTIES COME FROM?

POoR aims to create new opportunities, but the vast majority of jobs have come from clients approaching them directly, sometimes at community centres. At other times it puts forward a project to an institution they are trying to support with some positive work.

The Covid-19 pandemic brought in opportunities that POoR wouldn't have thought of before. After the initial culture shock, working from home has enabled them to take advantage of these. Less time spent commuting and being able to run their time more efficiently has given them greater capacity for their social enterprise work. They are now able to meet up daily (virtually) rather than just once a week in person.

NEW DIRECTIONS

POoR's aim is to be multidisciplinary as long as that serves its core mission. The founders are keen on trying different kinds of members with different skills, branching into different sectors, wherever their mission leads them.

At the moment, due to their background in architecture, they're receiving architectural commissions. In the future, they'll be thinking outside the architectural box, but always having one foot in the industry. Primarily their work isn't about architecture, it's about empowering young people. That can take many forms.

In the future, they believe they should be thinking about policy. They want to examine policies of how young people are being treated by the auditor of our generation. They will keep going back to their vision and mission and checking that new projects meet their values.

FIGURE 10.42 A young person painting a mural at Carney's Community Youth Centre

The three founders with an architectural background particularly enjoy working with Matt, whose job as an accountant gives him a unique perspective, one completely different to that taught at architecture school. They want to continue working with people in different industries to enrich the process.

ADVICE FOR OTHERS WANTING TO START UP

POoR would say that planning the business is crucial to starting out. It's important to understand what you want to be, what you want to achieve. Create a vision and a mission. As a collective they all have slightly different ideas, so deciding on their mission took 'some really thorough discussions, an intense moment lasting about three weeks'.

From this, they were able to create a vision, which is 'to create a world where youth see no limit'. Their mission is to develop communities through the elevation of youth. They find it incredibly useful having their mission decided rather than getting side-lined with projects that don't meet their values.

A couple times, Ben says they've been approached and been in slight danger of letting someone else define who they are. People will try and put you in a box to suit their agenda. It's important to spend a lot of time defining your purpose, so that you can resist people's attempts to put you in their own box.

After everything that happened with George Floyd and Black Lives Matter, POoR felt there was a sudden new pressure for companies to think about their social responsibility. Companies had wanted them to work on projects that really had nothing to do with their values. Their vision and mission came just in time.

HOPED-FOR CHANGES IN THE ARCHITECTURE INDUSTRY

POoR cares about how siloed the architecture industry is in general from the public. Larry feels that a lot of architecture appears to be for the architect, because we carry all the knowledge, we have a lot of say. The client doesn't have the expertise to deliver buildings, so they can be excluded from the design process – particularly in council estates. How can we enhance their ability to design? If we could bring their ideas out, we'd have much better designs. There's a lot more value in the client being able to take ownership and it isn't happening enough just yet. The RIBA Code of Conduct says: 'architects are there to serve the public interest'. Ben would really like to see that taken more seriously. Over 20% of the UK population is under 18, which is a large proportion to be let down by architecture. He'd like to see a reimagining of the core tenets of what it means to be an architect.

Shawn thinks that there's a lack of trust; sometimes it's actually better to pretend you're not the architect during a consultation, as people are more welcoming: 'We need to re-build that for more human- and people-centred work. If you think about Covid, for example, architecture should really be at the forefront of the discussion. I would expect that when Boris Johnson and Matt Hancock are speaking, you would have some kind of designer alongside them speaking about ways in which we can manage the distances of people, how our roads are going to be impacted how we navigate the city. But we don't really. If people could engage more with architecture, they would be more interested in what we do. We could regain a bit more power in the city as designers. This will take a long time to change because you're rebuilding from the ground up.'

This concrete vision combined with a flexible approach is inspiring. Many architecture practices could learn from POoR and design themselves into a much happier position, with clients, values and purpose all aligning. Super-niching, such as empowering young people, also lends itself to more lucrative work as you become a specialist (see more in Chapter 6 on marketing), so it makes good business sense too.

CONCLUSION

It's exciting to read about micro practices having a bigger impact by working with councils, collaborating, franchising or developing social enterprises. All have developed notoriety for their differentiators – not just one thing, more a combination of approach, styles and attitude that make each practice a unique offering to a client. Key learning outcomes from the last recession have led to building-in more financial resilience.

One might wonder if by diversifying practices we are suggesting that architecture does not offer enough on its own. I believe the opposite, that practices are providing extra value to clients and the world by diversifying. The world is changing very fast. It's up to us to change with it and understand what our clients will need from us. There are so many opportunities in these ever-changing times to flourish, to find niches and nooks within and outside the industry to specialise and grow. Architects are brilliant at pulling together multiple things or people and creating something spectacular. There will always be a place for us in the world; it's a question of how we want to develop.

NOTES

Chapter 1

1. Amy Cuddy, Ted Talk, 'Your body language may shape who you are'.
2. Cal Newport, *Deep Work: Rules for Focused Success in a Distracted World*, Grand Central Publishing, New York, 2016.

Chapter 2

1. Paul Oliver, *The Encyclopedia of Vernacular Architecture of the World*, Cambridge University Press, Cambridge, 1991 (latest edition: Dr Marcel Vellinga, The Encyclopedia of Vernacular Architecture of the World (2nd edition), Bloomsbury Publishing, UK, 2021.
2. Clare Nash, *Contemporary Vernacular Design*, How British Housing Can Rediscover its Soul, RIBA Publishing, London, 2016.
3. Cal Newport, *So Good They Can't Ignore You*, Piatkus, London, 2019.
4. Stephen Covey, *The 7 Habits of Highly Effective People*, Simon & Schuster, New York, 2017.
5. Seth Godin on the game of life, the value of hacks and overcoming anxiety (#476), Tim Ferriss podcast.
6. Adam Grant, *Originals: How Non-conformists Change the World*, WH Allen, London, 2017.
7. Dr Emma Hepburn, @the psychologymum, Instagram.
8. Stephen Covey, *The 7 Habits of Highly Effective People*, Simon & Schuster, New York, 2017.
9. Cal Newport, *Deep Work: Rules for Focused Success in a Distracted World,* Grand Central Publishing, New York, 2016.
10. https://www.theguardian.com/lifeandstyle/shortcuts/2018/dec/02/kids-always-want-to-stay-up-late-but-whats-the-optimum-time-for-them-and-you-to-go-to-bed

Chapter 4

1. SMART stands for Specific, Measurable, Attainable, Relevant and Time-bound. Using these headings ensures you have a very specific goal with measurable outcomes that is attainable (with effort/challenge), is relevant to your overall aims and is within a specific time frame.

FURTHER READING

Covey, Stephen, *The 7 Habits of Highly Effective People*, Simon & Schuster, New York, 2017

Ferriss, Timothy, *The 4-hour Work Week*, Vermilion, London, 2011

Gerber, M, *The E-myth Revisited: Why most small businesses don't work and what to do about it*, HarperBus, New York, 2001

Grant, Adam, *Originals: How Non-conformists Change the World*, WH Allen, London, 2017

Nash, Clare, *Contemporary Vernacular Design, How British Housing can Rediscover its Soul*, RIBA Publishing, London, 2016

Newport, Cal, *Deep Work: Rules for Focused Success in a Distracted World*, Grand Central Publishing, New York, 2016

Newport, Cal, *So Good They Can't Ignore You*, Piatkus, London, 2019

Northrup, Kate, *Do Less: A Revolutionary Approach to Time and Energy Management for Busy Moms*, Hay House Inc., California, 2019

Oliver, Paul, *Encyclopedia of Vernacular Architecture of the World*, Cambridge University Press, Cambridge, 1997 (latest edition: Dr Marcel Vellinga, Encyclopedia of Vernacular Architecture of the World (2nd edition), Bloomsbury Publishing, UK, 2021

Samuel, Flora, *Why Architects Matter: Evidencing and Communicating the Value of Architects*, Routledge, Abingdon, 2018

Schön, Donald, *The Reflective Practitioner: How Professionals Think in Action*, Basic Books Inc., USA, 1984

WEBSITES

EntreArchitect by Mark R. LePage https://entrearchitect.com/

Gardener, Chris, https://the3fs.com/

Hepburn, Dr Emma, @thepsychologymum, Instagram

The Business of Architecture by Enoch Sears, https://www.businessofarchitecture.com/

The School of Life, https://www.theschooloflife.com/, Campus LLP, London

SPEAKERS

Amy Cuddy, Ted Talk, 'Your body language may shape who you are'

Seth Godin on the game of life, the value of hacks and overcoming anxiety (#476), Tim Ferriss podcast

INDEX

Page numbers in **bold** indicate figures.

T

V

W

IMAGE CREDITS

Figure 1.1 Katie Reilly

Figure 1.2, 1.4, 4.1, 4.2, 4.6 (top, left), 4.7 (top, right), 4.9 (bottom, right), 5.5, 6.4 & 7.1 Luke Stevens

Figure 2.1, 2.2, 4.4, 5.1, 5.6, 9.1, 9.2 & 9.3 Julia Healey

Figure 4.5, 6.1 Sarah Birchall

Figure 4.8 (bottom, left), 7.2 & 7.3 Jaina Valji

Figure 5.3, 10.18 (bottom, right) Vivacious Mel Photography

Figure 10.1, 10.2, 10.3, 10.4 & 10.5 Office S&M

Figure 10.6 Katy Mutch

Figure 10.7, 10.8, 10.9 & 10.10 Harrison Stringfellow

Figure 10.11, 10.12 10.13, 10.14, 10.15, 10.16 & 10.17 Invisible Studio

Figure 10.18 (bottom, centre) Neil Rock

Figure 10.18 (top row & bottom, right), 10.20, 10.21 & 10.22 Transition by Design

Figure 10.19 Photograph by Dan Paton

Figure 10.23, 10.24, 10.25, 10.26 & 10.27 Gbolade Design Studio

Figure 10.28 Photograph by Peter Landers

Figure 10.29 Photograph by alma-nac

Figure 10.30, 10.31 & 10.32 Photograph by Jack Hobhouse

Figure 10.33, 10.34, 10.35 & 10.38 Photograph by Phil Tragen

Figure 10.36 Photograph by Lisa Raynes

Figure 10.37 Photograph by Beccy Lane

Figure 10.39 POoR

Figure 10.40, 10.41 & 10.42 Nick Cornwall